raptor!

raptor!

A kid's guide to birds of prey

Christyna & René Laubach
and Charles W. G. Smith

STOREY KIDS

The mission of Storey Publishing is to serve our customers
by publishing practical information that encourages personal independence
in harmony with the environment.

Edited by Deborah Burns and Anne Kostick

Art directed and designed by Wendy Palitz and Cynthia McFarland

Layout by Leslie Tane, Susan Bernier, Jennifer Jepson Smith, and Kelley Nesbit

Illustration and photo coordination by Ilona Sherratt

Photographs © Tom Vezo with exceptions as listed on page 116.

  Front cover of Red-tailed Hawk and back cover upper left photo of Turkey Vulture by
  Tom Vezo, back cover bottom photo by Giles Prett, and spine photo by Rolf Hansen

Illustrations by Chuck Galey

Raptor silhouettes by Ilona Sherratt

Maps and charts by Judy Sitz

Indexed by Susan Olason, Indexes & Knowledge Maps

Special thanks to Gus Ben David, director, Felix Neck Wildlife Sanctuary; Keith Bildstein, Ph.D., director of research and education, Hawk Mountain; Carl Burch, Zoological Supervisor, bird department, Miami Metrozoo; Peter Dubacher, director, Berkshire Bird Paradise; Rolf Hansen, Berkshire Bird Paradise; Tom Ricardi, Mass Birds of Prey; Jorge Zalles, Hawks Aloft education coordinator, Hawk Mountain; Teresa McHugh and Ananda Plunkett; and Richard Steege's sixth-grade class at Williamstown Elementary School.

Bird calls on pages 33, 36, 38, 42, and 44 are as described by David Sibley in *The Sibley Guide to Birds* (New York: Alfred A. Knopf, 2000).

The plans for the kestrel box on pp. 101–103 were rendered by Brigita Fuhrmann and originally appeared in *The Backyard Birdhouse Book* by René and Christyna M. Laubach (Storey Books, 1998). Craig Richardson built the box.

The information in this book is true and complete to the best of our knowledge. All recommendations are made without guarantee on the part of the author or Storey Publishing. The author and publisher disclaim any liability in connection with the use of this information. For additional information please contact Storey Books, 210 MASS MoCA Way, North Adams, MA 01247.

Storey books are available for special premium and promotional uses and for customized editions. For further information, please call Storey's Custom Publishing Department at 1-800-793-9396.

Printed in China by C & C Offset Printing Co., Ltd.

10 9 8 7 6 5 4 3 2 1

Library of Congress Cataloging-in-Publication Data

Laubach, Christyna M.
     Raptor! : by Christyna and René Laubach and Charles W.G. Smith.
          p.   cm.
     Includes bibliographical references (p.   ).
     Summary: Describes the physical characteristics, behavior, and different species of raptors.
     ISBN 1-58017-445-0 (alk. paper)
     1. Birds of prey—Juvenile literature. [1. Birds of prey.] I. Laubach, René. II. Smith, Charles
W. G. III. Title.
QL696.F3 L38 2002
598.9—dc21   2001054980

dedication

To the memory of Maurice and Irma Broun,

who taught so many to love and protect raptors.

Contents

Imagine you are a small animal,

minding your own business, scurrying low to the ground, going about your day. Suddenly you sense that something is watching you. You look around, but you don't see anything. Scary, isn't it?

Now imagine that whatever is hunting you has amazing powers. If you hide in the dark, it will find you, because its hearing is so good that it can hear your heart beating. Its eyes are so sharp that even when you can't see it, it can still see you. If you run, it will swoop out of the air, seizing you with talons so sharp that they'll puncture your back with the impact of a bullet. Once it has captured you, it will use its sharp hooked bill to tear you apart and eat you.

You, the small, scared prey, could be many different animals, such as a mouse, a bird, a cat, or a duck. But the incredible predator that hunts you can be only one thing: a raptor, possibly catching food for her hungry babies in the nest.

No matter where you live in North America, raptors are living nearby. Peregrine Falcons nest on skyscraper ledges in our cities; Bald Eagles and Osprey fish along our rivers and seacoasts; Turkey Vultures soar above farms and highways. And as night falls across the continent the owls awaken, in city, suburbs, and countryside, and begin their nocturnal quests.

Over millions of years, raptors have evolved to be the most efficient winged predators in the world. To survive they have to be stronger and faster and have sharper senses than their prey. The result is a group of birds with abilities that are truly astonishing.

Raptors are not just fierce, however; they are independent, intelligent, and loyal to their families. And they are important parts of a healthy ecosystem. Without them, for example, the numbers of rodents would rise dangerously to the point where they would not have enough food. There would be a massive die-off, and disease would spread. Like all predators, raptors are necessary to keep the natural world in balance.

In the following pages you will discover some of the reasons why raptors are among the most fascinating animals on the planet. You will learn where they like to hang out, how they fly, and what they look like. You will start hearing them at night, and you will recognize their calls during the day. You will even discover ways to help raptors survive.

Raptors are majestic, beautiful creatures, thrilling to watch and inspiring to learn about. Just knowing they are alive makes our hearts soar.

This is your personal guide to their exciting world.

Eye on you
A Red-tailed Hawk will spot you long before you spot it.

ONE
Raptors in Focus

A raptor is a carnivorous bird that feeds chiefly on meat taken by hunting or on **carrion** (dead animals), using its powerful talons to kill and carry its prey. The word raptor comes from the Latin word *rapere,* meaning to seize and sweep away. (Other words from the same root are "rapt," "enraptured," and "rapid.")

Although raptors are often called birds of prey, many other birds also hunt prey. Flycatchers nab flying insects; robins yank out worms. Flickers prey upon ants; pelicans scoop up fish. Raptors, though, are unique among birds because of their special survival tools.

Flying high
Eagles are masters of the air, the way great white sharks are masters of the ocean.

white-breasted nuthatch

Bird Basics

All birds share certain **traits**, or inherited characteristics, that make them birds and not snakes, snails, or monkeys. All birds have wings, beaks or bills, and two feet; all birds lay eggs. But other species have some of these traits as well. The one trait that belongs only to birds is feathers.

There are many different types of birds in the world, but songbirds, also called **passerines**, are often used as the model of a "typical" bird. Here's how raptors compare to songbirds:

● Both types have similar body parts: feet, feathers, wings, beaks, and eyes.

● Both vigorously defend their territory, especially during breeding season.

● Both pair off in long-term relationships. Songbirds remain with their mates for the entire breeding season; raptors stay together for the season or for life.

● Territory size differs greatly. A robin's territory may be only 1/10 of an acre (400 sq. m), while a Golden Eagle needs up to 60 square miles (250 sq. km) of home range to support itself and its family.

● Songbirds build new nests every year; raptors usually add to old nests, often for many years.

1

What Makes a True Raptor?

All raptors come with three features as standard equipment: powerful vision, sharp talons to grasp and kill prey, and a hooked beak to kill prey and tear it apart.

Many raptors have additional tools for catching their prey. Some, such as eagles, have great strength. Others, like owls, have very sensitive hearing, while still others, like falcons, are among the fastest flyers on the planet. Each raptor species has its own set of skills and tools that allow it to succeed where it lives.

Claws and Effects

A raptor's talons are very different from a songbird's claws. A sparrow's little claws are meant to scratch the dirt and cling to a branch. The large, powerful, curved, sharp talons of an eagle are designed to kill, to grip, and to carry heavy prey.

Unique Beaks

Each type of bird has evolved with a beak that helps it do special jobs. Osprey beaks have a hook to help them grip the fish that Ospreys eat. A Prairie Falcon has a notch in its beak, called a **falcon tooth,** which slips neatly between the neck bones of its prey. The bird kills its prey by breaking its neck. The Snail Kite's slender beak ends in a long hook, perfect for pulling snails out of their shells.

The raptor's nostrils are often located in the fleshy **cere**, which is often brightly colored and bare, to keep feathers out of the bird's nose when it breathes.

Just like our fingernails, raptors' beaks constantly grow, but they have a razor-sharp edge from constant use.

Gone fishing

Tail Winds

The tails of birds are used for many things, from attracting a mate to balancing on a perch. But raptor tails are especially good for steering in flight. The tail is composed of a group of feathers arranged in a fan.

Spread wide, the tail makes a larger sail area, which helps the bird soar better. If the tail is folded the bird can glide with speed. Turning the tail feathers steers the bird left or right. Some raptors that have fairly long, strong tails, like Sharp-shinned or Cooper's Hawks, can perform amazing tricks: loop-de-loops, rolls, and steep, blindingly fast dives. Often, two birds will perform a duet in the sky.

An Osprey will plunge right into the water after a fish. Occasionally the bird will drown when "hooking" a fish too heavy to be lifted.

Telling Tails

Raptors hold their tails open in a fan shape when soaring, twisted when turning, and closed when gliding or diving.

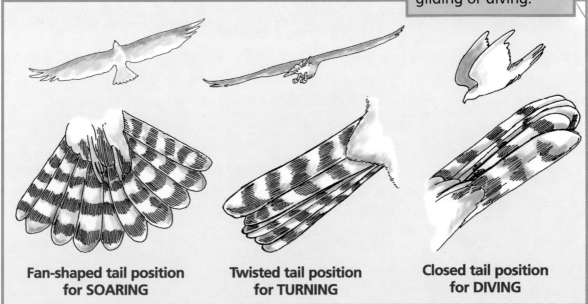

Fan-shaped tail position for SOARING   **Twisted tail position for TURNING**   **Closed tail position for DIVING**

What Big Eyes They Have

The eyes of some raptors are as large as people's eyes, but they look smaller because a large part of them is hidden. Raptors' eyes are much bigger than ours in relation to their heads.

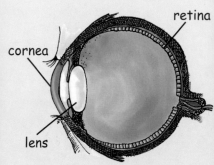

HUMAN EYE

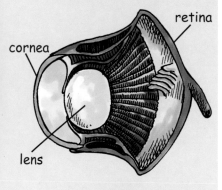

OWL EYE

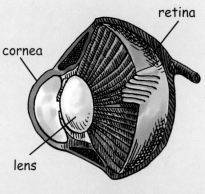

EAGLE EYE

The World's Sharpest Eyes

A raptor's eyes do just about everything better than ours do. Different species have different types of eyes, depending on whether they are active during the day **(diurnal),** like hawks, or at night **(nocturnal),** like most owls.

Day-Watching Eyes

Diurnal raptors need to see their prey clearly and in sharp detail from far away. In these birds both the cornea and the lens bulge more than in the eyes of other birds. This bulge allows them to focus better and to see more sharply.

The cornea and lens focus the image onto the **retina** at the back of the eye. The retina contains light-sensitive cells called **cones**. The more cones on the retina, the clearer the image appears. Diurnal raptors have huge numbers of cones, which produces color and clarity — much sharper than those of a human eye. In fact, a hawk's eyes are ten times more powerful than a human's.

Night-Watching Eyes

Nocturnal raptors (owls) need to see clearly in very dim light. Their eyes are tube-shaped and very large, to pull in as much light as possible. While the eyes of diurnal raptors have lots of cones, owls' eyes have lots of cells called **rods.** Rods allow nocturnal raptors to see well in very low light. In what we see as darkness, owls can see perfectly, but they are color-blind.

A Bird's Eye View

Most birds' eyes are set on the sides of their heads so that they can see more of their surroundings. This is called **monocular vision,** and it gives the bird a better ability to sense motion, such as the movement of a predator creeping up on it. Predators such as raptors, on the other hand, have their eyes set close together, on the front of their heads. The resulting **binocular vision** allows both eyes to focus on an object at the same time, creating **depth perception,** the ability to see in three dimensions (3-D). Depth perception lets the raptor see exactly where the prey is. When the raptor attacks, the talons hit their mark.

Cat's Eyes

Who else can see well at night? Scientists believe that domestic cats' night vision is as good as owls'. Also like owls, cats see only in black and white and shades of gray.

How Birds See

Binocular (two-eyed) vision occurs when the view from one eye overlaps the view from the other eye. Many prey birds, like pigeons, have eyes that can detect motion in almost a full circle. Owls, in contrast, look straight ahead the way we do.

two-eyed
(binocular)
vision

one-eyed
(monocular)
vision

Owl's Vision

two-eyed
(binocular)
vision

one-eyed
(monocular)
vision

one-eyed
(monocular)
vision

Pigeon's Vision

two-eyed
(binocular)
vision

one-eyed
(monocular)
vision

one-eyed
(monocular)
vision

Human's Vision

Soaring vs. Gliding

Soaring means a bird is staying level or going higher on rising air currents called thermals and updrafts.

Gliding means a bird is moving forward and level or down, with the help of gravity. In both cases, the bird needs to do very little or no flapping.

Flight

Raptors can fly in four ways: gliding, flapping, soaring, and hovering. Other birds can fly in one, two, or even three of these ways, but many raptors are experts in all four.

Gliding

This simplest form of flight was probably used by the earliest birds millions of years ago. A bird in a glide looks like an airplane coming in for a landing. The wings are tucked in slightly for speed, and the tail is

Above it all
This juvenile Ferruginous Hawk searches for prey from high in the sky.

closed, giving the bird a more streamlined shape, which helps it go faster. Raptors glide as they "stoop," or swoop down on prey. This gives them great body control to help them aim their talons accurately.

Flapping

When a bird flaps its wings in flight, the wings provide two different things at the same time: lift to keep the bird up and forward motion to keep it going.

Hovering

You may have seen a raptor hanging in one spot, its wings outstretched and motionless, like a kite in a breeze. Not surprisingly, this is called kiting, and the experts at it are called kites. Other raptors that kite include Red-tailed Hawks, Ferruginous Hawks, and Rough-legged Hawks.

In the other form of hovering, the bird's body is nearly vertical, suspended in the air, while its wings beat rapidly. Hummingbirds are the obvious champs here, but American Kestrels can often be seen hovering in this way over a clearing before dropping onto the prey below.

Soaring

Soaring means the bird is rising without flapping. To soar, a bird spreads its wings wide and fans its tail, creating a larger surface, or sail area, to catch the rising air or wind. True soaring uses about 1/20 the energy of flapping flight.

Raptors use rising columns of warm, upward-moving air, called thermals, and winds that bounce upward off mountain ridges, called updrafts (see page 8), to carry them skyward and forward.

1.

2.

3.

Causing a flap

1. A Red-tailed Hawk in flapping flight. The downstroke is strong and slow, the wings stretching out as if they are grabbing as much air as they can. The wings push down to lift the bird up but also reach forward to pull the bird through the air.

2. During the upstroke, the bird's wings sweep upward. In a split second the wing folds at the wrist and the front edge flips up.

3. The wings are fully raised and ready for another downstroke.

Thermals and updrafts are two types of air movements that raptors use to help them soar.

A **thermal** is a rising body of warm air. As the sun warms the earth each morning, the heated air near the ground begins to rise. Raptors, especially hawks and vultures, like to ride thermals, circling the outside edge of the rising current to climb higher.

Thermal

Updraft

An **updraft** is a wind that goes up and over an obstacle that it cannot go around. Updrafts often occur along unbroken ridges rising from long valleys. The wind currents can simply come up and over the ridge.

Raptors use thermals to travel. As the bird floats upward on the air, it will drift to the side, then turn around the outside edge of the air column. Once enough height is reached, the bird curves away and descends in a glide, picking up speed until it may be traveling at more than 60 miles per hour (96 kph). When it enters another thermal, it pulls up and rises some more. As its airspeed slows, it

Flight Patterns

resumes circling the edge of the thermal, slowly gaining altitude for its next glide. A raptor can fly a long distance this way without once flapping its wings.

Back to the Dinosaurs

Many scientists believe that the birds of today evolved from dinosaurs that lived millions of years ago. What kind of dinosaurs produced today's birds? No one is really sure. Scientists look for similarities between certain dinosaur fossils and today's birds. A group of dinosaurs called **coelurosaurs,** including the aggressive Velociraptor, has amazing similarities to modern birds and may be their long-sought ancestors. There is even evidence that some coelurosaurs had feathers, which makes the link between them and raptors even more likely.

The Dinosaur Connection

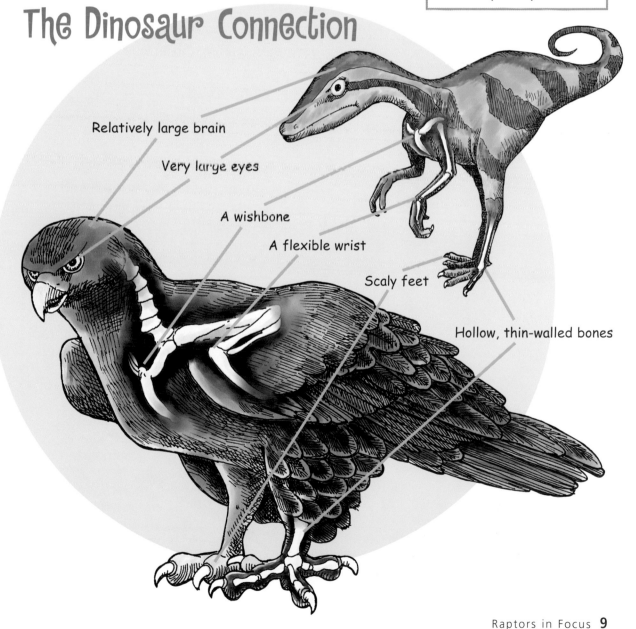

Relatively large brain

Very large eyes

A wishbone

A flexible wrist

Scaly feet

Hollow, thin-walled bones

Who's for Lunch?

Most animals, whether they are mice, songbirds, or grasshoppers, spend their lives always on alert for danger. That's how life is for most creatures. Their goal is to stay alive long enough to make sure their offspring — and therefore their species — will survive.

Balancing Act

Every **habitat,** or living area of a certain species, has a limit on the number of animals of each species it can support. A habitat always has more animals of a prey species than it has predators. This makes sense — if there were more predators than prey, there would soon be nothing for predators to eat. Prey species stay healthy because predators usually remove animals that are slow, weak, or not very alert, leaving the strongest to breed and continue the species.

One example of nature's balancing act is the relationship between Snowy Owls and their main prey, lemmings. Snowy Owls live on the Arctic tundra. Lemmings are small, furry rodents that also live on the tundra and multiply very fast. As the number of lemmings increases, their food supply (plants)

Food Pyramid

Food chains begin with the lowest form of life that is consumed by something else. A blade of grass is eaten by a caterpillar. The caterpillar is then eaten by a meadowlark, and the meadowlark is preyed upon by a hawk. If one link is removed, the chain is broken.

Snowy Owls need lemmings
Six-inch, mouse-like lemmings are the major part of a Snowy Owl's diet in the Arctic.

decreases because of all the hungry mouths. Meanwhile the number of Snowy Owls also increases because there is so much food around — the lemmings.

The lemmings increase in numbers for about four years, until there are lemmings everywhere and food for them nowhere. Soon enormous numbers of lemmings begin to die from starvation. As the lemmings die there is less food for the Snowy Owls, and some of them begin to die as well — but not all of them. Instead of starving in the Arctic, many Snowy Owls "pack their bags" and head south to find other rodents. So every four years or so the continental United States receives lots of Snowy Owl visitors from up north. Usually they stay in the northern states from New England to the Pacific Northwest, but they have been seen as far south as Texas.

&

lemmings need Snowy Owls
Without Snowy Owls, there would be so many lemmings that they would destroy most of the plants of the north country where they live.

A Day in the Life

On a May day while you are waking up, going to school, playing sports, using the computer, and going to bed, the raptors around you are also busy living their lives.

5:00 A.M.

Two **Red-tailed Hawks** open their eyes. The larger female stays with the three chicks as the male leaves the nest with a swoosh of feathers.

A **Great Horned Owl** returns from the night hunt to its nest in a pine tree, clutching a cottontail rabbit in its talons. Two downy babies peer at their supper.

6:00 A.M.

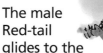

The male Red-tail glides to the top of a dead elm by a pond. Spotting a motionless chipmunk under a tree, he drops like a sword. The chipmunk scoots away, and the hawk breaks off the attack.

The Great Horned Owl roosts at the nest with its mate and their brood.

10:00 A.M.

The baby Red-tails are hungry, so both parents go hunting. As the male dives after a red squirrel scampering through the woods, the female flies ahead. The squirrel dodges the male by slipping around a tree, where it is met by the female's talons. Lunch is served.

The Great Horned Owl stirs. Its sensitive ears pick up the distant calls of crows. It becomes alert and swivels its head to survey its surroundings. Then it settles its feathers and closes its eyes.

The female Red-tail soars on a thermal high above a hayfield, searching for prey. The male stays near the nest.

The owl family rests in its nest in the tree.

6:00 P.M.

The male Red-tail leaves its mate and young at the nest in its last search for prey this day.

The adult owls continue to rest, waiting for dusk and their time to hunt. The young grow restless.

9:00 P.M.

The Red-tails fly back to their nest and settle among the babies.

The male Great Horned Owl awakens and floats from the nest to a tree near the edge of a field to watch the night.

MIDNIGHT

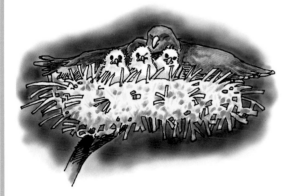

The Red-tails are asleep in their nest.

The female owl leaves the nest and silently glides toward a rabbit nibbling some grass. Without slowing, she lifts it with her strong talons and carries it back to her young. They devour the rabbit.

1:00 A.M.

The two Red-tailed Hawks open their eyes. It is "owls' light," when both diurnal and nocturnal raptors are quiet.

TWO

Close-up & Personal

All raptors have certain things in common. That's what makes them raptors. But they have lots of differences, too. To find and watch these magnificent predators it is helpful to know the similarities and differences among them. Learning about the different birds of prey — where they live and hunt, how they fly and take care of their young, the sound of their calls, and what they eat — helps deepen appreciation and respect for them. After you have watched for a while you will be able to identify a species from far away, simply by the way it soars or the shape of its silhouette.

vulture   osprey   kite   northern harrier   golden eagle   harris hawk

Family Resemblance

To organize and make sense of the world, scientists place all living things in groups with their closest relatives. One set of scientific groupings is called a family (which scientists give a Latin name ending in "-idae"). By studying the kind of DNA in each species, scientists are now looking backward through evolution to find out how all living things, including raptors, are related to each other.

When you spot a bird of prey in the sky or perched in a tree, you can figure out whether it is an eagle, vulture, or hawk if you know a few facts about the different raptor families.

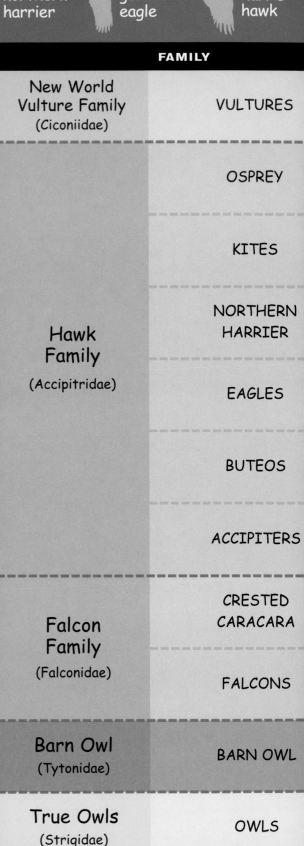

FAMILY	
New World Vulture Family (Ciconiidae)	VULTURES
	OSPREY
	KITES
Hawk Family (Accipitridae)	NORTHERN HARRIER
	EAGLES
	BUTEOS
	ACCIPITERS
Falcon Family (Falconidae)	CRESTED CARACARA
	FALCONS
Barn Owl (Tytonidae)	BARN OWL
True Owls (Strigidae)	OWLS

sharp-
shinned
hawk

northern
caracara

american
kestrel

barn
owl

great
horned
owl

What It Looks Like	Hunting Style	Flight Facts
Large to very large size. Dark color. Weak feet and talons, hooked beaks, small, naked heads.	Eat mostly carrion	Soar
Long, narrow wings held in an M-shape. Feet have sharp tubercles to hold prey.	Eat live fish	Dive feet first for fish
Pointed wings (first primary is noticeably shorter than others), long, flared tails, slim.	Swoop and dive to catch, feet first, insects, mice, lizards, frogs	Buoyant flight
Long wings with rounded tips, wings held in slight V-shape, long tails, owl-like face.	Hunts mice, rats, and frogs partly by sound	Hunts by flying close to the ground; long, slow turns
Very large size. Dark color. Long, broad wings, wide tails.	Sharp eyes; eat fish, small mammals, snakes, birds, and carrion	Soar
Medium to large size. Long, broad wings, fan-shaped tails.	Extraordinarily keen eyesight	Soar
Small to large size. Relatively short wings, long tails.	Eat birds caught on wing	"Flap, flap, glide"
Large head, long neck and legs, naked red face.	Eats carrion	Soar
Long, narrow, pointed wings bent back at wrist, long tails, notched (toothed) bills.	Hunt insects, reptiles, and small mammals	Stoop on prey; some hover before plunging
Large head, heart-shaped face, eyes fixed in sockets (can turn head 270 degrees), white below, rusty above, very sharp talons, hooked beaks.	Nocturnal, hunts small mammals by sound	Silent flight
Very small to very large size. Large heads, round faces, eyes fixed in sockets (can turn head 270 degrees), very sharp talons, hooked beaks.	Mainly nocturnal, hunt small mammals mostly by sound	Silent flight

how it looks: Blackish brown, almost eagle-sized, with long wings and tail and small naked head, red in adults and gray in juveniles. Wings below are two-toned black and silver-gray; tail below also silvery. Holds wings up in V when soaring and rocks back and forth when gliding.

length/ wingspan: 26" (66cm)/ 67" (170cm)

call: Usually silent; can hiss

habitat: Open areas, farms, woods, roadsides, ridges

migration: As far south as South America; many winter in southeastern U.S. *Spring peak:* March to April *Fall peak:* October to November

favorite food: Almost any type of dead animal (carrion)

Summer breeding range

Year round range

Turkey Vulture
Cathartes aura

The most common large birds of prey in most of North America, Turkey Vultures are often seen soaring and rocking on thermals and updrafts. Unlike Black Vultures, Turkey Vultures find carrion by smell as well as sight. They frequently feed on roadkill. Vultures' weak talons don't usually allow them to catch and kill live prey. They roost in trees or on cliffs at dusk and nest on bare ground on cliffs, in caves, and in hollow logs and empty buildings up to 20' (6.2m) high. Most adults have only one mate each year. *Common.*

how it looks: Large, black, smaller than Turkey Vulture (but heavier), with stubby black tail and stocky, short dark wings with silvery gray near tips. Head is small, gray, and without feathers.

length/wingspan: 25" (64cm)/59" (150cm)

call: Usually silent; can hiss

habitat: Open areas, garbage dumps, roadsides, chicken farms, fishing piers

migration: Some birds move south from northern part of range in winter, but few birds actually migrate. *Spring peak:* April to early May *Fall peak:* October

favorite food: Carrion; may catch small birds and mammals

Black Vulture

Coragyps atratus

While most raptors make flying look easy, Black Vultures look like they're still learning. They hold their wings nearly flat when soaring and, unlike Turkey Vultures, they flap a lot. Look for groups feeding on roadkill or in roosts at dawn and dusk. Black Vultures will kill prey and chase Turkey Vultures from carrion. These vultures use sight, not smell, to find food. They nest on bare ground or in caves, hollow logs, stumps, or thickets. Adults usually have one mate each year, and family groups stay together all year. *Common.*

Year round range

how it looks: Very large with long, graceful wings; white below and dark brown above. White head with blackish face patch. Wings bent at wrist (along middle of front edge), like those of gulls. Black patch visible on underside of wing near wrist.

length/wingspan: 23" (58cm)/63" (160cm)

call: Series of loud whistles: *tewp, tewp, tewp*

habitat: Lakes, rivers, and coastal areas

migrates: Alone or in small flocks. *Spring peak:* late March to May *Fall peak:* late September to October

favorite food: Live fish

Summer breeding range

Year round range

Winter range

Osprey

Pandion haliaetus

Also called "fish hawk," the Osprey is the only raptor that dives feet first into the water after prey. It always holds fish with the fish's head forward. Its talons are long and sharp, and its toes are rough to hold onto slippery fish. Bald Eagles sometimes chase Ospreys to steal their fish. Ospreys are found flying over coastal marshes and large rivers and lakes. An Osprey nest is a large mass of sticks, mud, and other materials atop dead trees or human-made objects like bridges and utility poles, 10' to 60' (3–18.3m) up. Adults have only one mate each season. *Common; increasing.*

how it looks: Small raptor, slightly larger than a pigeon, with dusty gray body, grayish white head with black eye patch, and notched black tail. Body and wings similar in shape to those of a falcon.

length/wingspan: 14" (36cm)/34" (86cm)

call: High, thin whistle: *pee-teeew,* second part lower

habitat: Open woodlands near streams, ponds, and swamps; dry rangeland

migration: Migrates in flocks to central South America. *Spring peak:* April *Fall peak:* early September

favorite food: Large insects (grasshoppers, dragonflies)

Mississippi Kite

Ictinia mississippiensis

These birds often hunt in flocks, grabbing flying insects in their talons and eating them while flying. While flying, this bird noticeably twists its flared tail as it switches direction in the blink of an eye. Unlike the White-tailed Kite, the Mississippi Kite doesn't hover. Large flocks can often be seen passing through Texas on their way to and from South America each year. Kites raise their young in loose colonies, building compact nests of sticks lined with green leaves and sometimes Spanish moss in tall trees 30–135' (9–42 m) up. Adults normally have only one mate each year. *Common; increasing.*

Year round range

how it looks: Large, with dark blue-black wings and back and white head and belly. Tail long and dark with deep fork. Wings long, slender and falconlike.

length/wingspan: 22" (56cm)/50" (127cm)

call: Short, high whistles: *klee-klee*

habitat: Coastal wetlands, swamps, open woods

migration: In flocks to South America. *Spring peak:* late February to early March *Fall peak:* late August to early September

favorite food: Large insects, lizards, nestling birds

Year round range

Swallow-tailed Kite

Elanoides forficatus

Watching the Swallow-tailed Kite fly will give you goose bumps. This southern raptor dips and banks, swoops and dives through the sky while plucking insects from the air and small lizards from the trees. It drinks by skimming the surface of the water. Identify a Swallow-tailed Kite by its long, deeply forked tail and white head. It builds nests of twigs lined with grass and Spanish moss in treetops 60–130' (18.5–40m) up. Adults usually have one mate each year. *Uncommon; declining.*

White-tailed Kite

Elanus leucurus

The White-tailed Kite can be identified by its pointed wings, black wing tips, and bright white tail, easily seen when the bird is soaring. When cruising over grass-lands and marshes looking for rodents, this raptor often hovers (unlike any other North American kite) before suddenly dropping onto its prey. Like other kites, it is an excellent flyer with long easy glides and sharp turns. *Common; increasing.*

Year round range

how it looks: Graceful medium-sized hawk with long tail and wings and an obvious solid white patch on its rump. Males are gray above and white and chestnut below. Females are brown above. Unlike other hawks, harriers have owl-like faces that help them listen for prey.

length/wingspan: 18" (45cm)/43" (109cm)

call: Sharp, high-pitched whistle *eeeya* or high *sseeew;* male makes dry barking sound *chef chef chef* or *kekekeke*

habitat: Open places like fresh or saltwater marshes, fields, and prairies

migration: Migrates alone, in pairs, and in small flocks. *Spring peak:* mid-February to early June *Fall peak:* early August to late November

favorite food: Small mammals (especially voles), amphibians, reptiles, small birds, insects, carrion

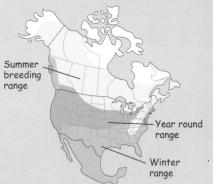

Summer breeding range

Year round range

Winter range

Northern Harrier

Circus cyaneus

The Northern Harrier, once called the Marsh Hawk, is a bird of open, often wet places like marshes, fields, and wet meadows. Harriers often flap-and-glide as they cross back and forth over the hunting area, rocking on slightly upraised wings. They bank through turns slowly, almost stalling before picking up speed again. Unlike most daytime raptors, Harriers use hearing to find prey. When they do find it, they drop out of the air like stones onto their victims. Harriers sometimes use a low perch, but they more often hunt from the air. *Common but declining.*

adult male

juvenile

how it looks: Very large dark brown raptor with fawn-gold crown, back of neck, and base of tail below. Wings long, head looks fairly small, tail dark with darker end band. Young birds have tails that are white at the base and black at the end.

length/wingspan: 30" (76cm)/79" (201cm)

call: High-pitched, fairly weak *keeep-keeep*

habitat: Mountains, hills in open country

migration: Migrates alone or in pairs; some do not migrate. *Spring peak:* March *Fall peak:* November

favorite food: Jackrabbits, small mammals; also eats birds, reptiles, insects, carrion

Golden Eagle

Aquila chrysaetos

Golden Eagles are about the size of Bald Eagles but have a personality all their own. While Bald Eagles would rather take an easy meal, Goldens are much more likely to hunt for their own food. These powerful raptors soar high, their wings held in a shallow "V," searching for prey below. When a meal is spotted, Goldens attack in a long, amazing swoop. Look for Golden Eagles soaring along ridges or near their nests, which are often at the very edge of cliff ledges. *Uncommon to common; stable or increasing.*

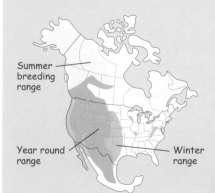

Summer breeding range

Year round range

Winter range

how it looks: Very large black-brown raptor with white head, huge yellow bill, and white tail. Young birds are dark, often mottled with white. A young Bald Eagle looks something like a young Golden Eagle, but the young Golden's tail is sharply two-toned with white and black.

length/wingspan: 31" (79cm) (northern birds larger than southern birds)/ 80" (203cm)

call: Weak, squeaky whistles *kleek, kik-kik-kik*

habitat: Seacoasts, rivers, and large lakes

migration: Migrates alone or in pairs; winters along coasts from Alaska and Newfoundland south and along water bodies in interior U.S. *Spring peak:* March *Fall peak:* November

favorite food: Fish (dead or alive); also ducks and geese, rabbits, carrion

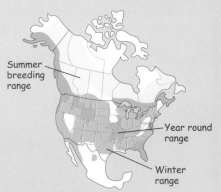

Summer breeding range

Year round range

Winter range

Bald Eagle
Haliaeetus leucocephalus

Seeing a Bald Eagle for the first time is a thrill you'll never forget. This bird is huge with very long dark wings held in a straight line like an airplane. It often soars in wide circles on updrafts and can be identified from a long distance when sun reflects off its white tail as it turns. It often hunts from perches such as shoreline trees where it stays for long periods. Bald Eagles are easily seen near their huge nests, which are reused year after year. U.S. National Bird. *Uncommon to locally common; increasing steadily.*

how it looks: Small hawk (male is size of a blue jay, female slightly larger than a pigeon) with long, squared-off, banded tail. The wings are wide and short and held forward when gliding and soaring, making the head look small. The flight style of Sharp-shinneds is usually a few quick flaps, then a glide, followed by more quick flaps.

length/wingspan: 12" (30cm)/23" (58cm)

call: Sharp *kee-kee-kee*

habitat: Coniferous and mixed forest

migration: Alone or in small flocks, as far south as Panama *Spring peak:* Mid-March to mid-May *Fall peak:* September to October

favorite food: Songbirds

Sharp-shinned Hawk

Accipiter striatus

Sharp-shinned Hawks aren't very big, but they're bold and fearless predators. Their favorite prey are songbirds that they nab on the wing after an often acrobatic and dizzying chase through thick vegetation. They are most easily observed in winter when they hang out near bird feeders. In the warmer months "Sharpies" are often harder to observe. They can regularly be seen, often in large numbers, at migration viewing points across the continent. *Common; declining in eastern North America.*

Summer breeding range

Year round range

Winter range

how it looks: Crow-sized hawk similar to Sharp-shinned Hawk but with longer tail; adult has dark grayish brown back and chest with rusty stripes. Young bird has brown back with brown streaks on breast and belly. Tail is banded with black and white below and has a wider white tip than does Sharp-shinned Hawk.

length/wingspan: 17" (43cm)/30" (76cm)

call: Loud, barking *kek, kek, kek*

habitat: Mixed forest broken with meadows or clearings, especially near streams

migration: Some migrate alone or in small flocks as far as Central America. *Spring peak:* mid-March to mid-May *Fall peak:* September to October

favorite food: Songbirds, small mammals

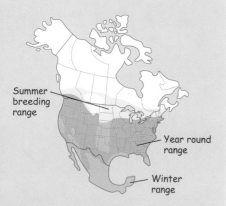

Summer breeding range

Year round range

Winter range

Cooper's Hawk

Accipiter cooperii

Cooper's Hawk is a bigger twin of the Sharp-shinned Hawk with similar ranges, markings, and habitat. In flight Cooper's usually holds the front edge of its wings in a straight line, while the Sharp-shinned holds its wings more forward, forming a "U" shape near the head. Also, the Cooper's tail usually appears rounded at the end, while the Sharpie's often looks square. Cooper's Hawks are secretive and uncommon so observing these quick, acrobatic predators is a challenge. Like Sharpies, they are most easily observed during fall migration at hawk watching sites. *Uncommon; increasing.*

Harris's Hawk

Parabuteo unicinctus

This raptor of the central and south Texas brushlands and desert Southwest has the look and fearless glare of a Golden Eagle but with very beautiful markings all its own. These birds often seem tame and can be seen perched on fence posts and utility poles along road-sides. Harris's Hawk often hunts in small family groups, so if you see one bird, watch for others nearby. They fly low over their hunting territory, patrolling back and forth over the same area, and sometimes can be seen feeding on roadkill or other dead animals. *Uncommon; declining; reintroduced in some areas.*

how it looks: Large hawk with chocolate brown body highlighted by reddish brown shoulders, under-wing linings, and upper legs. Tail is black and white.

length/wingspan: 20" (51cm)/44"(112cm)

call: Raspy-sounding *keh* repeated many times

habitat: Desert and mesquite brush lands

migration: Does not migrate

favorite food: Small mammals, rabbits, snakes, birds, insects

Year round range

Broad-winged Hawk

Buteo platypterus

During September thousands of migrating Broad-winged Hawks a day may sail along Appalachian ridges to the oohs and aahs of delighted birders. Broad-winged Hawks have just one wide white stripe on the tail, while the similar Red-shouldered Hawk has several narrow ones. When not migrating, Broad-wingeds are shy and usually stay in thick woods below the treetops. When hunting they are bolder and can often be seen perched on poles or wires along wooded roads. They usu-ally swoop down on prey from a perch. *Common.*

how it looks: Our small-est buteo, this crow-sized, stocky hawk has a dark brown back and white chest, marked with rusty barring. In flight, from underneath, the wings look whitish, with black edging. The tail shows one broad white band between two black ones.

length/wingspan: 15" (38cm)/34" (86cm)

call: Thin, sharp, two-note whistle, *pe-heeeee*, the sec-ond note higher (sometimes imitated by blue jays)

habitat: Deciduous (some-times mixed) woods, often near pond or stream

migration: Often in large flocks. *Spring peak:* April to early May *Fall peak:* mid- to late September

favorite food: Rodents, reptiles, amphibians, insects, young birds

Summer breeding range

how it looks: Medium-sized hawk; adult has white chest and belly horizontally barred with rust-orange. The back and top of wings are dark with a flash of orange on each shoulder. The tail is black with narrow white stripes. Florida birds are lighter colored.

length/wingspan: 19" (48cm)/40" (102cm)

call: Loud, slightly grating *keee-yeeuur* given several times; imitated by blue, Steller's, and maybe also gray jays

habitat: Deciduous and mixed forests near streams, wooded swamps

migration: Alone or in small flocks. *Spring peak:* March to early April *Fall peak:* October

favorite food: Small mammals, reptiles (especially snakes), amphibians (mostly frogs), insects, small birds

Red-shouldered Hawk

Buteo lineatus

Also called the Swamp Hawk, the Red-shouldered Hawk usually stays in the forest and only occasionally comes to perch at the edge of meadows and fields. It is most often seen perched on a low branch at the edge of a wooded swamp, waiting for the chance to drop onto any prey that wanders below. Near the end of each wing is a curved whitish patch, called a "window," visible on bright days as the bird flies overhead. It is more common to hear the call of these birds than to see them. *Fairly common; declining.*

Summer breeding range

Year round range

Winter range

how it looks: Large, classic-looking hawk, dark above and light below, with rust-orange tail. In West can range from nearly black to very pale. Most have a dark brown "belly band" below their creamy white chests. From below, they show dark patches on the front edges of their wings, near their shoulders. Young Red-tails have brown-banded tails.

length/wingspan: 19" (48cm)/48" (122cm)

call: Sharp, raspy scream – *keeeerrr* – that starts high and shrill, then trails off

habitat: Forest, edge habitat, prairies, fields and meadows, desert

migration: Only northern populations migrate, alone or in small flocks, to more southern parts of range. *Spring peak:* late March *Fall peak:* early November

favorite food: Rodents; other small mammals; birds, reptiles, amphibians, insects

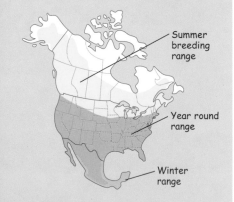

Summer breeding range

Year round range

Winter range

Red-tailed Hawk

Buteo jamaicensis

The Red-tailed Hawk is the most common hawk in North America and lives in more habitats than any other raptor. It is often seen perched on utility poles along roadsides and atop tall dead trees. Red-tails most often hunt by swooping down from a perch and by flying over meadows and fields. In normal flight the birds most often flap three to five times, then glide. Red-tails often soar and climb quickly into the sky on thermals and updrafts. As they make wide circles, their fanned red tails are often very visible. *Common; increasing.*

Swainson's Hawk

Buteo swainsoni

Swainson's Hawk soars with its wings held up in a very slight "V" and sometimes rocks side to side in the wind a bit like a Turkey Vulture. In flight, the white wing linings stand out against the blackish wing feathers. This large, slim hawk often hunts in a group and can be seen on the ground stalking prey from grasshoppers to prairie dogs. Swainson's likes to fly low and will kite above prey before attacking, but it will also use perches for hunting when available. Migration takes place in small groups that join to form very large flocks as the birds pass into Central America. *Common.*

Juvenile

how it looks: A slender raptor almost as large as a Red-tailed Hawk. Comes in two colors, light and dark. Light-colored birds are dark brown above, with a white face, reddish brown chest, and white belly. The gray tail has one thick black band near edge. Dark birds have a dark brown face, chest, and belly.

length/wingspan: 19" (51cm)/51" (130cm)

call: Long, scream – *kwee-oaaah* – higher and weaker than Red-tail's

habitat: Prairies, deserts, open rangeland, farm fields

migration: Migrates in flocks to grasslands of southern South America. *Spring peak:* April to May *Fall peak:* late September to mid October

favorite food: Mostly small mammals, insects; also rabbits, reptiles, amphibians, and young birds

Summer breeding range

how it looks: Large hawk with long wings; black patches at tips are visible when bird flies overhead. White tail has wide black band near tip. Can be light or dark. Light birds have black belly (darkest in young birds) and white breast streaked with brown; dark birds are blackish (the young bird has a lighter head).

length/wingspan:
22" (56cm)/53" (135cm)

call: Whistle-like *keeeerrr*

habitat: Tundra, open spruce forest, prairies, fields, meadows, marshes

migration: Alone and in small flocks. *Spring peak:* April *Fall peak:* November

favorite food: Rodents; insects

Summer breeding range

Winter range

Rough-legged Hawk
Buteo lagopus

The Rough-legged Hawk spends its summers on the Arctic tundra and in open spruce forest and is seen by most people only in winter when the birds come to spend the coldest months in milder parts of North America. These big hawks like to fly slow and low on up-turned wings over fields and meadows, often hovering before dropping onto prey. They choose perches near the ground and when in trees often grip slender twigs that look too weak to hold them. Their small beaks and feet help them retain heat in the far north. *Uncommon.*

how it looks: Nearly eagle-sized with rusty back and upper wings (dark brown in young birds); under parts, including flight feathers, mostly white with light rusty tail. Legs covered to talons with rust-colored feathers. Rare dark form almost all deep reddish brown with light-colored flight feathers.

length/wingspan: 23" (58cm)/56" (142cm)

call: Loud whistled *kreeeaaah*

habitat: Prairies, dry scrub, badlands

migration: Short distance migrant; stays year-round in some areas

favorite food: Ground squirrels, jackrabbits, prairie dogs; also snakes, large insects

Ferruginous Hawk

Buteo regalis

The common name of this, our biggest and heaviest buteo, is due to its rusty iron color but might also have to do with its great strength. The Ferruginous Hawk is a raptor of the open plains and dry lands of western North America. It can be seen flying over prairie dog towns where it often kites before swooping down on prey. Ferruginous Hawks hunt from perches where available; open habitat and the hawk's large size together make it easy to see perched birds. *Uncommon; may be declining over much of its range.*

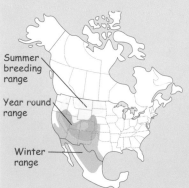

Summer breeding range

Year round range

Winter range

how it looks: Large, dark brown bird with long white neck and black cap on head, heavy bill, and very long yellow legs and feet. Bare skin of face is red. Wings are dark with white tips; wide and rounded like a vulture's. Tail white underneath with black tip.

length/wingspan: 23" (58cm)/49" (118cm)

call: Cackling *grrrrk;* alarm call *kek, kek, key*

habitat: Dry open brushlands and prairie; also wetter areas; will nest in palmetto, cactus, and other trees

migration: Does not migrate

favorite food: Carrion; also small mammals, insects, reptiles, crustaceans, fish, turtle eggs, and almost whatever it can find

Year round range

Crested Caracara
Caracara cheriway

While most raptors are famous for being great flyers, the Crested Caracara is good at running. This large and striking bird of prey is related to the falcon but sure doesn't look like one. Crested Caracaras are most often seen on the ground as they stalk prey or run after it. Look for their very long legs and large, thick bill. They are also commonly seen flying up and down roads in the morning looking for roadkill. They will chase vultures from carrion. Mexican National Bird. *Locally common; declining.*

American Kestrel

Falco sparverius

The American Kestrel is the smallest hawk in North America and one of the most common. You can observe this robin-sized falcon along highways and near farm buildings. Kestrels, our only cavity-nesting diurnal raptor, often hunt from perches on electrical wires, utility poles and low tree branches along roadsides and fields. When it spots prey, the bird leaves its perch and hovers above its target before diving onto it in a lightning-fast attack. It can be recognized by its small size and rusty orange back and tail. *Common; declining in some areas.*

how it looks: Small falcon with slender body, long tail, and sleek, tapered wings. Male's wings are blue-gray above, pale orange-white beneath. Female's wings are rusty above. Back and tail are rust-colored with black tip on tail in male. Female has rusty tail with brown barring. Face has two dark sideburns — one in front of and one behind each eye.

length/wingspan: 10" (25cm)/22" (56cm)

call: Sharp and piercing *killy-killy-killy*

habitat: Open areas from farm fields and grasslands to city parks

migration: Migrates in small flocks as far south as Panama; many winter in U.S. *Spring peak:* late March to early May *Fall peak:* September to October

favorite food: Insects, small mammals, reptiles; also birds in winter

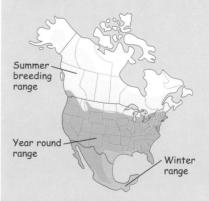

Summer breeding range

Year round range

Winter range

how it looks: Small, dark, stocky falcon with bluish gray or brownish gray upper parts (females and young are brown) and under parts streaked with rust and white. Wings short and pointed, tail long and boldly banded in black and white. Has a faint dark streak below its eye.

length/wingspan: 11" (28cm)/24" (61cm)

call: Fast *twitwitwitwitwit-wit* that speeds up, gets higher, then lower

habitat: Prairies and grasslands, open coastal areas, marshes

migration: Most migrate; some as far as northern South America; birds on Canadian Prairies move closer to cities in winter. *Spring peak:* March to May *Fall peak:* September to October

favorite food: Birds in flight; also small rodents, large insects

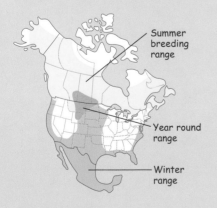

Summer breeding range

Year round range

Winter range

Merlin

Falco columbarius

Like the legendary wizard of the same name, the Merlin is so skillful at catching prey that it sometimes seems like magic. Merlins are small, powerfully built, aggressive falcons that are very good at nabbing birds and dragonflies out of the sky. Merlins swoop into a flock of birds, separate a slower bird from the rest, and chase it down with a burst of speed. They do not hover or dive on prey, but they often fly fast and low. Merlins are most easily seen along the East Coast in the fall when northern populations follow their prey, songbirds (especially warblers), south. *Uncommon; may be declining.*

Prairie Falcon

Falco mexicanus

The Prairie Falcon may seem edgy because it is quick to chase off intruders and always appears to be in a hurry. Look for this aggressive raptor perched on shrubs, on fence posts, or high up rock faces. When chasing birds, Prairie Falcons fly low and fast, streaking just above the grass or scrub to flush their prey. It works. Prairie Falcons glide more than soar and fly with quick but stiff wing beats. They also stoop and hover for prey. *Uncommon to common; declining in some areas.*

how it looks: Large falcon, the size of a Peregrine, with light brown upper parts, a pale chest spotted with brown (strongly streaked with brown in young birds), and mostly pale under wing color. Only raptor to show dark brown areas at base of under wings ("wing pits"). Wings are rounded at tip; tail is long, pale, and faintly banded. Thin brown sideburn below eye and white eyebrow above.

length/wingspan: 16" (41cm)/40" (102cm)

call: harsh *kree-kree-kree*, like Peregrine's but higher

habitat: Prairies, desert mountains, and plains

migration: Most do not migrate; some winter on Great Plains and south along West Coast

favorite food: Birds in flight, small mammals, insects, and lizards

Year round range

Winter range

how it looks: Large falcon with blue-gray upper parts and barred belly and wings. Tail is short and marked with narrow bands. Bold black sideburn beneath eye makes it look as if it is wearing a helmet.

length/wingspan: 16" (41cm)/41" (104cm)

call: Harsh *rehekk, rehekk*

habitat: Open areas near coast, rivers, cliffs, and sky-scrapers

migration: Some migrate as far south as southern South America. *Spring peak:* March to early May *Fall peak:* October

favorite food: Birds in flight (in cities, especially pigeons)

Peregrine Falcon

Falco peregrinus

The fastest living thing on earth, this raptor can reach speeds of 100 miles (160 km) per hour as it dives towards prey. Peregrines like to fly high in the sky and have a straight, fast flight with rapid but strong wingbeats. When prey is seen, the bird often drops into a headfirst dive called a power-stoop, striking feet first and often instantly killing the prey. *Uncommon; endangered.*

Summer breeding range

Year round range

Winter range

how it looks: Medium-sized owl with heart-shaped white face and dark brown eyes; sometimes called "monkey-faced" owl. Has rusty and gray upper parts and white or pale rusty underparts (males are whiter below). Feathers look soft, like pillow stuffing, and are dotted with shiny specks that resemble sequins.

length/wingspan: 16" (41cm)/42" (107cm)

call: Harsh, hissing, scary shriek *cssshhtt*

habitat: Open areas near human habitation, farm fields, meadows, towns, cities; deserts; nests in cavities, usually in barns, silos, or steeples; will accept nestbox

migration: Does not migrate except in very northernmost part of range

favorite food: Rodents; birds, bats, reptiles; helpful in controlling mice and rats around barns

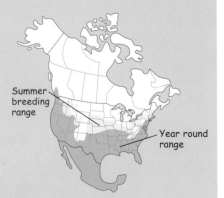

Summer breeding range

Year round range

juvenile

Barn Owl

Tyto alba

The Barn Owl is often called the ghost owl for its dead-of-night habits, silent flight, pale color, scary-sounding voice, and fondness for old buildings and cemeteries. The Barn Owl has the best hearing of any owl and can even hear a mouse walking across a hard floor from about 100 feet (30 m) away. These long-legged raptors have adapted to life near people and are most often seen in open areas near barns or vacant buildings. Barn Owls nest in any month of the year, even winter. *Uncommon to rare; declining.*

Short-eared Owl

Asio flammeus

Short-eared Owls are more at home in the air than any of the other owls are. Like the Northern Harrier that it resembles, the Short-eared Owl is most often seen at dawn and dusk, flying low over marshes and wet meadows, hunting voles (meadow mice) and other rodents. To tell the two birds apart, watch how they fly. Short-eared Owls have a bouncy flight while Northern Harriers fly in a straight line. This owl will sometimes hover before dropping feet first on prey. If an adult is bothered near its nest it will pretend to have an injured wing, to draw intruders away. *Fairly common; declining.*

how it looks: Crow-sized owl with long, narrow wings, cinnamon-brown above and buff streaked with brown below. Stocky body; has dark marks like sunglasses around yellow eyes. Tiny ear tufts usually hard to see.

length/wingspan: 15" (38cm)/38" (97cm)

call: Male gives soft, widely spaced *pooh...pooh...pooh;* also makes barking sounds

habitat: Prairies, grasslands, tundra, fresh and saltwater marshes

migration: Northern birds migrate to U.S.

favorite food: Voles and other small rodents; also songbirds, insects

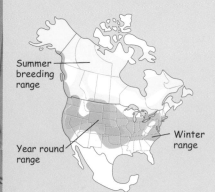

Summer breeding range

Year round range

Winter range

how it looks: Medium-sized, slender owl with mottled gray-brown body, streaked below, not barred like Great Horned. Long straight ear tufts, rusty brown face, and yellow eyes. When perched, wings stick out past tail. Looks something like a small, thin Great Horned Owl.

length/wingspan: 15" (38cm)/36" (91cm)

call: Males give soft *wooip* call; females say *she out*. Both say *bwak, bwak*

habitat: Thick woods near open areas and water

migration: Some migrate south as far as northern Mexico

favorite food: Small rodents; some birds

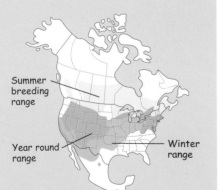

Summer breeding range

Year round range

Winter range

Long-eared Owl
Asio otus

Long-eared Owls are masters of disguise. Their mottled feathers look like tree bark, and they can stretch their bodies to look just like a broken branch, then perch very still for long periods. The result is a bird that is very hard to spot. In winter Long-eared Owls often roost in the same tree, close to the trunk, for many days in a row. Sometimes flocks roost together. To find the birds, look for owl pellets under dense evergreen trees in winter. *Uncommon.*

Great Horned Owl

Bubo virginianus

juvenile

The Great Horned Owl has the largest range and is probably the most powerful owl in North America. Crows, sometimes joined by Red-tailed Hawks, often mob it. A night hunter, it is also seen at dawn and dusk perched in a tree or other lookout. It hunts from perches or while flying close to the ground. Its pellets are large, about 4 inches (10 cm) long, and pile up under its roost in dense evergreens. Great Horned Owls are well known as fearless hunters and will attack large animals and people who try to climb up to their nests. They are called "hoot owls" in some areas. *Common.*

how it looks: Very large yellow-eyed owl with stocky body, large head, and obvious ear tufts. Feather color varies a lot; Pacific Northwest birds are the darkest; tundra-edge birds of central Canada are the lightest. Also, females are usually browner and more heavily marked than males, who tend to be paler.

length/wingspan: 22" (56cm)/44" (112cm)

call: Loud, but muffled series of *hoo-hoo-whoo-hoo-hoo* ("Who's awake? Me, too!")

habitat: Very wide variety, from forests to deserts to city parks; nests in tree cavity or large abandoned nest of hawk or squirrel

migration: Does not migrate

favorite food: Rabbits, rodents, skunks, birds as big as grouse and herons; also reptiles, amphibians, insects

Year round range

how it looks: Large, stocky owl with round head (no ear tufts) and very dark brown eyes. Cream-colored upper breast is barred with brown, lower breast and belly streaked with brown, tail banded. Upper parts are brown mottled with white.

length/wingspan: 21" (53cm)/42" (107cm)

call: Loud series of hoots ("Who cooks for you, who cooks for you all?"); also a wide variety of barking and cackling sounds. May hoot in daytime, unlike other owls

habitat: Evergreen and mixed forests and swamps

migration: Does not migrate

favorite food: Mice, shrews, squirrels, rabbits; also crayfish, amphibians, reptiles

Year round range

Barred Owl

Strix varia

Barred Owls are very talkative and naturally curious. They will often answer even poor imitations of their calls with booming hoots and sometimes even come to investigate. This makes Barred Owls one of the easiest night-time raptors to hear and even see. During the day, Barred Owls like to rest in stands of cool, dense evergreens or mixed woods near water. If disturbed they often fly just a short distance before perching again. Barred Owls hunt rodents from perches. *Common; expanding.*

how it looks: Large dark-eyed owl with dark brown feathers spotted with white. Looks like the Barred Owl but is slightly smaller and has white spots instead of brown bars on chest.

length/wingspan: 18" (46cm)/40" (102cm)

call: *Whup hoo-hoo-hoooo*

habitat: Old-growth evergreen forests, shaded canyons; nests in tree cavity, cave, or abandoned hawk's nest. Habitat severely reduced by logging

migration: Does not migrate, except sometimes up and down mountains

favorite food: Rodents; also rabbits and squirrels

Spotted Owl

Strix occidentalis

The Spotted Owl lives in old open forests with large trees and hunts by dropping down from a perch onto its prey. More than 90 percent of its habitat has been cut down, causing a big drop in the Spotted Owl's numbers and lots of concern about its future. It is a secretive bird that prefers to live in the deepest, most isolated parts of the forest. It spends the day resting on a branch in thick cover. The Spotted Owl sometimes mates with the Barred Owl. *Endangered.*

Year round range

how it looks: Large white owl with round head, yellow eyes, and no ear tufts. Males can be nearly pure white, females and first year birds speckled with dusky brown. Our heaviest owl.

length/wingspan: 23" (58cm)/52" (132cm)

call: Deep *hoot brrrowww;* also bark (male) and quack (female)

habitat: tundra; airports, other open areas in winter

migration: Irregular migrant in winter to northern states; rarely as far as southern U.S.

favorite food: Lemmings, rodents; birds

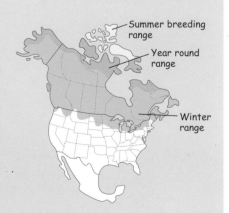

Summer breeding range

Year round range

Winter range

Snowy Owl

Nyctea scandiaca

The Snowy Owl's round head, widely set eyes, and comical feathery mustache make it appear as if it is just about to ask you a question. The only white owl in North America, the Snowy Owl is best seen during winter in open areas like beaches, airports, or fields. It is often active during the day and likes to perch on the ground, fence posts, buildings, or other higher spots in open spaces. Since it blends in with snow, it can be hard to see. It is most often found south of Canada during years when the population of lemmings (its favorite food) declines. *Fairly common to rare.*

Eastern Screech-owl

Otus asio

The Eastern Screech-owl is small, but because it often lives in or near towns and cities and calls a lot, it is one of the most familiar owls of eastern and central North America. Although Screech-owls do not screech, the song of this little raptor, often heard in movies, is a spooky whinny that may send chills up your spine. The calls are fairly easy to imitate. During sunny winter days Eastern Screech-owls often perch at the entrance of a tree cavity, but usually their color and pattern are a perfect camouflage. Screech-owls are the only small owls with long ear tufts. *Common; declining.*

how it looks: Small owl with yellow eyes and ear tufts that can be flattened against the head, making it look round. Comes in different colors, from cinnamon red to slate gray, with some a brownish mix of the two. Gray is most common overall.

juvenile

length/wingspan: 8.5" (21.5cm)/20" (51cm)

call: Spooky, shrill whinny; also a whistled trill

habitat: Open woods, parks, suburban and city backyards with large trees

migration: Does not migrate

favorite food: Insects, small mammals, amphibians, birds

Year round range

how it looks: Small owl almost identical to Eastern Screech-owl with yellow eyes and ear tufts that can be flattened against the head. Western Screech-owl has darker bill than Eastern. Feathers mostly gray with some brownish birds along the Pacific coast.

length/wingspan: 8.5" (21.5cm)/20" (51cm)

call: Series of whistles that sound like a bouncing ping-pong ball; sometimes a two-part trill

habitat: Open woods (especially oaks), streamside trees, desert, parks, and suburban areas; nests in abandoned woodpecker holes and will accept nestboxes

migration: Does not migrate

favorite food: Small mammals, insects, spiders, amphibians, reptiles, birds

Year round range

Western Screech-owl

Otus kennicottii

Western Screech-owls look a lot like their eastern cousins but have some differences. For one thing, they sound different. Though Western Screech-owls are often heard at night, they are harder to track down and observe than Eastern Screech-owls. During the day these night-time raptors often perch in the entrance of a tree cavity, sunning themselves, but are hard to see since they look so much like broken-off dead branches. Western Screech-owls like to stay in one place, or territory, for months at a time, so if you do see one the chances are pretty good it may be there tomorrow, too. *Common.*

Elf Owl

Micrathene whitneyi

The smallest owl in the world, this tiny raptor can fit in the palm of your hand. During the day these birds rest in an old woodpecker cavity in a tree, giant cactus, or telephone pole, and at night they hunt insects. Elf Owls depend a lot on woodpeckers to make cavities that they can later use for roosting and nesting. This owl's coloration is also excellent camouflage making it very difficult to see even from a short distance. In winter Elf Owls migrate from the southwestern states to central Mexico and return in spring. *Common; endangered in California.*

how it looks: Sparrow-sized owl with a small round head and yellow eyes. Speckled gray back, with brownish gray and white face and underparts. Tail is very short. Resembles Northern Saw-whet Owl but is smaller and has no streaks on underparts.

length/wingspan: 5.75" (15cm)/13" (35.5cm)

call: High-pitched yips and puppy-like barks

habitat: Saguarro cactus desert and oak, pine, and sycamore trees near water; nests in abandoned woodpecker holes

migration: Short distance migrant from southwestern United States to north-central and central Mexico

favorite food: Insects, scorpions, spiders, centipedes, shrews, mice

Summer breeding range

Year round range

Winter range

how it looks: Very small reddish brown or grayish brown owl with yellow eyes and dark false eye spots on back of neck and tiny white spots on top of the head. The underparts are white, the sides are the same color as the back, and the belly has blackish streaks. The long tail has black and white bars.

length/wingspan: 6.75" (17cm)/12" (30cm)

call: Long series of double or single *too* notes

habitat: Dense pine-oak woods in foothills and mountains

migration: Does not migrate except for birds in southeast Alaska

favorite food: Birds (as big as Mourning Doves), small rodents, insects

Winter range

Year round range

Northern Pygmy-owl

Glaucidium gnoma

This small owl doesn't have eyes in the back of its head, but it looks as if it does. The Northern Pygmy-owl is tiny, but still a fierce hunter. To scare off predators it has two dark eye-like spots on the back of its neck. You can often find Northern Pygmy-owls during the day by watching songbirds. When songbirds find a roosting owl they mob it until it moves away. While most owls fly silently, the wings of these make a whirring noise. They hunt mostly at dawn and dusk, not at night. *Fairly common.*

Northern Saw-whet Owl

Aegolius acadicus

The little Northern Saw-whet Owl was given its odd name because its call sounds like a carpenter's saw being whetted, or sharpened. When they are singing, the birds often answer peoples' imitations of their song by singing faster. Northern Saw-whet Owls are active at night and hunt mice and other rodents from perches. During the day, as they roost on a low branch in thick cover, they can be approached very closely. They are active strictly at night, even when migrating. *Uncommon to fairly common; rare in most of winter range.*

how it looks: Very small owl with rusty-red or reddish gray upper parts and white underparts heavily streaked with reddish-brown. "V"-shaped white eyebrows and yellow eyes.

length/wingspan: 8" (20cm)/17" (43cm)

call: *Toot toot toot* in long series

habitat: Evergreen or mixed forest and bogs

migration: Migrate alone or in small flocks as far as southern U.S. *Spring peak:* April *Fall peak:* late October to early November

favorite food: Small rodents; also birds, insects

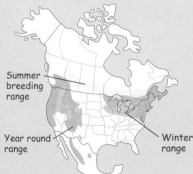

Summer breeding range

Year round range

Winter range

how it looks: Small owl with long legs and short stubby tail. Brown body is speckled and barred with white. The head is small with yellow eyes and no ear tufts.

length/wingspan: 9.5" (24cm)/21" (53cm)

call: Male – high-pitched sad-sounding *coo-coo-coooo*. Female – *eeep* call; also barks and screams

juveniles

habitat: Prairies, grass-lands, golf courses, airports

migration: Many west-ern birds migrate as far south as Central America; most others do not migrate

favorite food: Insects; also rodents, lizards, birds

Summer breeding range

Year round range

Winter range

Burrowing Owl

Athene cunicularia

The Burrowing Owl is one of the easiest and most fun owls to observe. Though it hunts mostly at night, it can often be seen during the day standing on the mound of soil outside its burrow or on a fence post. When people or predators come too close, these owls bow up and down before ducking underground to safety. Burrowing Owls can also imitate the rattle of an upset rattlesnake as a way of scaring away predators. The best places to observe Burrowing Owls are near golf courses, airports, and active prairie dog towns. *Locally common; declining.*

THREE

Watching
the Watchers

Raptor Watcher's Pack List

Things to take along on a raptor-watching expedition include:

- notebook and pencil
- binoculars
- *Raptor!*
- proper shoes and clothing for conditions
- water and food
- sunblock and bug repellent
- camera (optional)

There is an old saying that for every hawk you see, three more are watching you. After you've watched raptors a while, you'll begin to see them everywhere. You'll understand their habits and behavior, and you'll be able to guess where and when your next sighting may occur. You'll even be able to tell one kind of hawk from its close relatives.

Be a Top Spotter

Practice will make you a better raptor spotter. During migration periods, scan the skies every minute or so until you spot a bird; at a long distance, they may look like dark specks. After finding one, bring the binoculars up to your eyes without taking your eyes off the moving bird. Focus and check shape, size, way of flying, color and pattern, and anything else that you can see.

Choose Your Tools

The best binoculars for beginners are 8 x 40, meaning that they magnify things eight times and that the diameter of the large lens (the **objective**) is 40mm. Over time you can increase the magnification. Look for binoculars that are not too heavy, since you may have them hanging around your neck for hours.

Watch Your Manners

Being watched can make us feel uncomfortable, and it's the same with birds. They are very aware of what goes on in their territory, and disturbances may make them abandon their nests and nestlings or even leave the area completely.

10 Tips for Spotting Raptors

1. Look up frequently!

2. Be extremely quiet.

3. Watch the weather for best conditions.

4. Head for the hills: Watch raptors along their migration routes.

5. Look on trees and telephone poles.

6. Check fields and meadows, where raptors love to hunt.

7. Watch near water: Bald Eagles, kites, and Ospreys like shoreline habitat.

8. Listen! If you hear a raptor call, it must be close.

9. Stroll just after dark to hear and see owls.

10. Join local bird groups and go raptor watching with experts.

Watching the world go by
From its perch on a farm windmill a Harris's Hawk in Tucson, Arizona, looks for prey.

highway

city

farm

Where the Birds Are

You can find raptors almost anywhere, but certain places are better than others. September, October, March, and April are usually the best months to watch migrating hawks, and 10 A.M. to 3 P.M. is usually the best time. Weather makes a big difference, too. See Resources for a list of where and when to watch migrating raptors and information on Websites that track migrations.

Roadside Supervisor

Many raptors like to hang out along the side of a road and see what wanders by. Kestrels, for example, often survey the world from electric and telephone lines, while Red-tails perch atop dead roadside trees. Look up into

the sky to see soaring vultures on the lookout for tasty roadkill. Utility towers are another place where raptors are likely to watch and wait for prey.

Field Work

Farms, pastures, and open fields are good places for raptors to find rodents and other animals. Barn Owls are especially helpful in controlling the mice and rats on a farm. Barn Owls nest in old barns, Turkey Vultures soar overhead, and Kestrels and Red-tailed Hawks cruise the fields or survey them from open perches like utility poles and lines. Many raptors, including falcons, hawks, eagles, Short-eared Owls, and Northern Harriers, visit meadows and prairies. Look for them circling high above or cruising low over open areas.

meadow

Dead trees

Cooper's, Sharp-shinned, Rough-legged, and Red-tailed Hawks often perch on dead trees at the edges of forests.

On the Edge

Edge habitat is the place where one kind of habitat meets another kind, such as where a forest meets a field. Edge habitats attract many types of animals, both prey and predator. Raptors like to cruise along the boundary or sit in tall trees at the edge, looking for prey. Hawks prefer the dead trees, while owls like both live and dead ones. If the edge habitat borders water, look for kites, ospreys, and eagles cruising over the water, soaring above it, or perched in shoreline trees.

Going Up

Ridges and cliffs often create updrafts, those wind currents that help raptors soar. Buteos (including Broad-winged Hawks), eagles, and vultures are the most likely raptors to be seen soaring on updrafts.

The concrete canyons of cities have become good habitat for raptors, especially Peregrine Falcons. These birds like the plentiful supply of pigeons and the lofty ledges of skyscrapers for nesting. With binoculars or a spotting scope you may be able to see nesting falcon pairs. Cities with large areas of green space may also attract larger raptors, like Red-tailed Hawks, that may even nest there.

Being a Good Guest

When you enter a raptor's territory, try to act like a well-mannered guest. Here are some guidelines:

◆ Do no harm — protect the wildlife and the environment at all times. Be as invisible as possible; be quiet, don't step on sticks, and do not damage vegetation. If you must speak, speak quietly.

◆ Do not approach or disturb nests, roosts, feeders, or other sensitive areas. How close you can get depends on the species of bird you're watching. Too close is when your actions change the behavior of what you are watching; with raptor nests, 300 feet (92 m) is close enough.

◆ Do not touch, pick up, or attempt to feed birds or other animals.

◆ Avoid loud noises and jerky, unpredictable behavior.

◆ Respect private property.

◆ Do not leave trash; the area should be as pure and clean when you leave as it was when you arrived. Carry your trash back home with you.

Raptor Locator

If you see a raptor... ...it is likely to be a(n)...

If you see a raptor...	it is likely to be a(n)...
soaring overhead	vulture, buteo, eagle, golden eagle, red-tailed hawk, osprey, kite
on a tall city building or high ledge	peregrine falcon
on a metal or wooden utility pole	buteo, kestrel, golden eagle, red-tailed hawk
in a live tree, especially an evergreen	owl
on an electric line	buteo, kestrel, red-tailed hawk
on a dead tree, telephone pole, or fence post	vulture, buteo, kestrel, golden eagle, red-tailed hawk, rough-legged hawk, falcon, northern harrier, bald eagle, osprey
in an open field	vulture, buteo, eagle, golden eagle, owl, red-tailed hawk, falcon, northern harrier, short-eared owl, bald eagle, kite
at the edge of a water habitat	kestrel, golden eagle, owl, northern harrier, short-eared owl, bald eagle, osprey, kite

Column headings (left to right): vulture, buteo, eagle, peregrine falcon, kestrel, golden eagle, owl, great horned owl, red-tailed hawk, rough-legged hawk, falcon, northern harrier, short-eared owl, bald eagle, osprey, kite

3 Steps to Using Binoculars

Fitting. Binoculars are hinged so that you can adjust them to your own eyes. Hold the binoculars up to your eyes. If you see two images, move the two halves out or in (at the hinge) until the images become one.

Finding. First look directly with your unaided eyes at the object you want to see better. Imagine a straight line between your eyes and the object. Then, without moving your head, bring the binoculars up to your eyes so that they point along the line between your eyes and the object.

Focusing. When you have centered the object in the binoculars, close your right eye and turn the focus dial on the middle of the binoculars until the image is sharp. Open your eye. Now close your left eye and turn the focus dial on the right lens until you have a perfectly clear picture.

8 x 40?

This measurement looks like a multiplication problem. The first number is the magnifying power. The second number is the diameter, in millimeters, of the large lens (called the objective) farthest from the eye. So "8 x 40" means that objects will look eight times larger and that the large lens is 40 mm wide.

The lenses of many binoculars are coated to cut down on reflections and improve contrast and brightness.

Many binoculars have rubber eye cups around the small lenses (**oculars**). If you wear glasses you can roll the eye cups down and put the binocular lenses right up against the lenses of your glasses.

A good pair of binoculars has independent focus dials. The one on the middle of the binoculars focuses both sets of lenses (this is the one you use to focus the bird); the one on the right lens focuses only the right set. This one needs to be adjusted only once.

Migration

In the northern hemisphere, birds fly south in fall to wintering grounds, where they can escape the cold and find plenty of food. In spring they fly back to their northern range to breed and raise their young. In the southern hemisphere, it's the opposite: Birds fly north for the winter. Some birds even fly from one hemisphere to the other. Some raptors, such as Turkey Vultures, are short-distance migrants, with only a few hundred miles separating their wintering areas from their breeding grounds. Others, such as Ospreys, are long-distance migrants and travel thousands of miles each fall and spring.

As raptors migrate south in fall, they often ride **cold fronts,** masses of cold air from Canada. As the front races south it produces powerful updrafts ahead of it that can launch a raptor into the air at more than 30 miles per hour. Many birds, such as Red-tailed Hawks, seem to wait for the first strong cold front of the season to begin their southerly travels. You can often predict when large numbers of birds will appear in fall by checking a weather map in the newspaper, on the Internet, or on television. Be on the lookout in the fall for a cold front on the move.

Best Hawk-Watching Time

Between late August and mid-November, hawk watching can be especially good when:

1. A cold front is predicted.
2. Winds are from the northwest.
3. The temperature is dropping.
4. The humidity is decreasing.
5. The sun is warming the ground to produce thermals.

Flyways and Skyways

People use highways to travel from one place to another, and so do migrating birds. Their highways are called **flyways** and often follow land features such as mountain ranges, major rivers, and coastlines.

Different types of raptors sometimes show a preference for certain flyways. Buteos, such as Broad-winged Hawks and Swainson's Hawks, prefer the inland routes that follow north-south mountain ranges and river valleys, because they need thermals and updrafts for soaring. Accipiters and falcons, including Cooper's Hawks and American Kestrels, usually travel along the coast where their food (small birds) is likely to be. Species that don't migrate long distances, such as vultures and kites, seem to wander around rather than follow flyways. In general, migrating raptors follow their prey species.

Map Key

WEST

CENTRAL

EAST

SOUTH

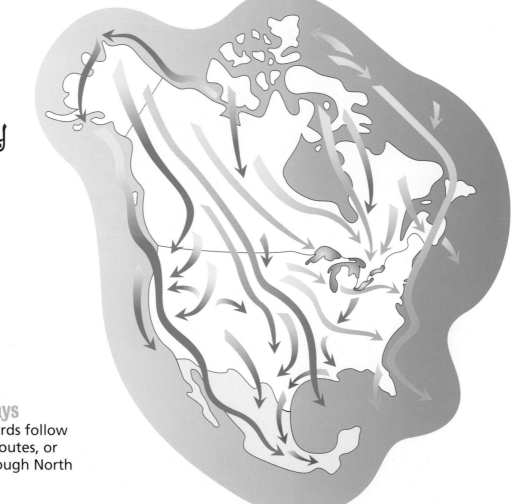

Sky highways

Migrating birds follow four major routes, or flyways, through North America.

Roadside raptors

For the last 14 years we have been straining our eyes to count every raptor we can during car trips between western Massachusetts and the Midwest. Instead of counting state and provincial license plates or playing other games to pass the time, we decided to see how many birds of prey we could spot from our car while traveling at highway speeds.

So far, we have counted 3,445 raptors (a total of 13 raptor species) while driving 25,200 miles (40,940 km), enough to circle the globe at the equator! That is about one raptor every seven or eight miles (12 km) of interstate highway.

Nearly four out of every five raptors counted were Red-tailed Hawks. This isn't surprising since Red-tails are big and like to perch along the grassy borders of highways where there are plenty of rodents. American Kestrels came in second and were one-fifth of the hawks spotted. Kestrels too use the grasslands along the roads for hunting.

We have seen Short-eared Owls in Hamilton, Ontario, and a tiny Saw-whet Owl perched just inside the tree cover in New York State. A real wintertime treat is the occasional Snowy Owl or the wintering Rough-legged Hawks hovering over fields of corn stubble or perched on fence posts in Ohio. Roadside raptor counting is a lot of fun and helps drivers stay awake too — but they should keep their eyes on the road!

At home

Bald Eagle males and females are similar, except the females are larger. They both take care of their babies.

FOUR

Life Among the Raptors

Nesting territories must provide all the comforts of home: everything a pair of birds will need to raise their young. This includes a place to mate and nest, safety from predators and competitors, and plenty of food.

Defense System

If another bird should enter a raptor's territory, most often the raptor will dive-bomb the invader, often from behind. Aiming at the back or the head, a raptor will slam the intruder with spread talons and sometimes take a swipe with open beak as well. Some raptors, such as Great Horned Owls, will also attack people to protect their mates and young.

All mine

Many raptors will stand over a fresh kill, spreading their wings and fanning their tails to hide it from competitors. This is called **mantling.**

Sky Dancing

If you see two raptors fly high into the sky and then dive and soar at one another, you may be witnessing a courtship dance. Each species dances differently: Bald Eagles dive toward each other and lock talons, then spiral down through the air for many seconds before letting go. Red-tailed Hawks repeatedly dive at each other in fake battles, briefly lock talons, and fill the air with their haunting cries. Other sky dancers are the Northern Harrier, the White-tailed Kite, and the Ferruginous Hawk.

When mating, in late winter to early spring, the male balances on the back of the perched female. The reproductive organs of raptors are inside an opening called the **cloaca,** and the balancing act is designed to bring the cloacas of the two birds together. The male keeps his feet balled up tight during mating so he won't hurt the female with his talons. As a result, he often loses his balance and falls off the female's back.

Pairing off
When two birds are sky dancing high overhead it can look as though they are fighting.

Back off
A raptor's **threat display** is its signal that you (or another competitor) are too close. It spreads its wings and puffs its feathers up to look as big and tough as possible. If you see this, walk away immediately, because the bird may attack.

Home sweet home
Eagles and Ospreys build huge nests that they return to each year. Some Bald Eagle nests have been in continual use by different pairs for as long as 30 years and are the largest tree nests in the world.

1 Egg or 2?

Large raptors, like Turkey Vultures, tend to lay one or two eggs, while smaller birds, such as Kestrels, lay the most eggs, between four and seven.

Raptors don't lay all their eggs the same day. Usually a single egg is laid every two or three days. The eggs hatch at different times, so the older hatchlings have a survival advantage over their brothers and sisters.

Bald Eagle egg

Nests and Nestlings

The nests of raptors range from holes in trees to nearly bare scrapings on the ground to huge structures of sticks weighing more than a ton. The most common style of raptor nest is made of sticks; each year the returning birds add more sticks to it. A nest of sticks sounds pretty uncomfortable, but the place where the eggs rest, called the cup, is lined with softer material like grass.

Some raptors don't even build nests. Great Horned Owls will use old nests made by hawks, crows, or even squirrels.

When baby raptors hatch, they can't do much more than eat and sleep. Their mother keeps them warm and protects them while their father brings back food. Many male raptors prepare the meal by tearing the prey into little pieces that the baby birds can handle. The nestlings don't remain helpless for long and within three weeks are restless and moving around in the nest.

Flight School

Baby raptors aren't born knowing how to fly. Each one must be taught. The young birds start by exercising their wing muscles while still in the nest. Young raptors, called **fledglings**, spend a few weeks exercising their wings while perched on branches near the nest. This is called **branching.** After that, while the fledglings are learning to fly and hunt, the parents continue to bring them food. Before the summer ends most fledglings can take care of themselves on their own.

Branching out
Young Barred Owls perch on a branch as they begin learning how to fly.

Dinner is served
A Red-tailed Hawk presents prey to its young.

On the Hunt

The types of prey hunted by different raptors include fish, snails, insects, songbirds, gamebirds, shorebirds, waterfowl, snakes and lizards, raccoons, rodents, crustaceans (like crayfish), and earthworms. To hunt such a wide array of animals, raptors have developed hunting methods designed especially for whatever type of prey they are after.

Some owls, buteos, and falcons most commonly hunt from a perch such as a telephone pole or a dead tree. The bird looks for movement and listens for sounds that tell it that rodents or other prey animals are nearby. When the bird spots its prey, it sharpens its attention, launches itself from the perch, and swoops down on its target.

Raptors sitting on a perch aren't always hunting, however. Sometimes they're just relaxing. A bird that is just watching the world go by will have its body feathers slightly fluffed, giving it a soft airy look. When a bird is looking for prey, its feathers are flat against its body, giving it a sleek appearance.

Searching for prey
A Crested Caracara looks and listens for prey from its perch in a dead tree.

No mercy
Whatever the prey, raptors like this female Northern Harrier are some of the most efficient predators on the planet.

Mob Justice?

In the world of raptors and songbirds, the raptors often win. Nobody ever hears of a chickadee preying on a Sharp-shinned Hawk. But songbirds have their revenge for being snack food when a number of birds gather around a raptor and harass it until they drive it away. It's called **mobbing.**

In the usual mobbing situation, the raptor is perched and seems to be minding its own business. The mobbers will gather around the raptor, screaming alarm calls while staying a safe distance away. Sometimes the mobbing birds will try fake attacks on the raptor, but through it all the predator most often just sits there as if nothing is going on or flies away to a quieter spot.

Nothing beats the show put on by crows, Red-tailed Hawks, and Great Horned Owls. When a flock of crows sees a perched Great Horned Owl, they will descend in a cawing mass to harass it, keeping up the racket until the raptor flies off. As it flies away it is common to see one or two Red-tailed Hawks trailing after the crows. The hawks don't harass the owl or bother the crows. They just seem to follow along and watch. In the end the owl loses patience with the game and outdistances the crows.

Hawking

Raptors that prey on large flying insects or birds are excellent at **hawking,** or seizing prey on the wing. They attack the prey as it flies, grasp it in their talons, and fly on with dinner in hand (or foot). Experts at hawking include accipiters, kites, and especially falcons.

Swallow-tailed Kites hawk eggs from other bird's nests by swooping past an unguarded nest, grabbing the egg in their talons, and flying off again, all in the blink of an eye.

Working together

Small birds can sometimes chase a raptor away from their nests by banding together and attacking in an aggressive group, a type of behavior called mobbing.

Flying High

The highest flying bird is Rueppell's Griffon (a vulture from Africa), which can reach altitudes of at least 37,000 feet (11,385 m). How do we know? Because an airliner hit a Rueppell's Griffon at exactly that altitude in 1973.

Vulture Culture

Vultures are raptors, too, but they have an image problem: Some people don't think that they are very attractive, and they smell bad, too (at least to humans). And their lifestyle might even be described as . . . creepy. But vultures, like other raptors, are masters of a special set of incredible skills: finding dead or dying animals, and soaring. Just imagine what the world would be like without vultures!

Dead Right

Like other raptors, vultures use their sharp eyesight to find food. The Turkey Vulture is the only one that locates food by smell as well as by sight. Once food is found, they use their hooked beaks to pull and tear flesh from the dead body. Their talons are fairly weak.

Though vultures are known as scavengers, they sometimes get tired of waiting for nature to take its course, so they go out and kill something to eat.

Don't Frighten a Vulture

When vultures are startled, they throw up all over everything nearby, to lighten themselves before taking off and maybe to scare off what's bothering them. As you can imagine, vulture vomit is pretty disgusting.

Into Thin Air

Vultures wobble awkwardly when they walk, but they are the very best of all birds at soaring. This helps them survive. Soaring uses less energy than flapping, so vultures need fewer calories per day than other birds do, and thus they can survive longer when food is scarce.

Soaring also allows birds to find food with less effort: Turkey Vultures can concentrate on seeking the odor of decomposing flesh to find carrion. And when soaring as high as 10,000 feet (3,000 m), they have a view of about 100 square miles (250 sq. km) and can watch other soaring vultures far below searching for food. When a low-flying vulture finds food and descends, its fellow vultures at higher levels follow it down and share an easy meal.

The More the Merrier

Vultures are sociable birds who often hang out in groups ranging from a few birds to many dozens. During the day they can be seen soaring in wide circles through updrafts and thermals. At dusk they descend to communal (group) roosts, often a dead tree or rock ledge. Seeing dozens of vultures perched in a dead tree at twilight is definitely a memorable experience.

The roosts are used day after day, and they are not pretty places. Vultures are big birds and not very neat, so in no time the tree and ground are covered with big, white droppings.

Easy rider
While many birds must flap their wings regularly to stay aloft, vultures have it easy. They use rising air currents and their large wings to keep them soaring with a minimum of effort.

Suited for the job
Turkey Vultures have very few feathers from the neck up, which makes it easier for them to plunge their heads deep into **carrion** (dead animals).

A Year in the Life

The seasons of a raptor's life revolve around finding a mate, building a nest, laying eggs, raising babies, and finding food. Each species has its own life style.

A human family in southern Ontario places some wood shavings in an **American Kestrel** nesting box they built. They bring the box to a field and fasten it to the trunk of a straight solitary dead tree, hoping a pair of kestrels will nest here in the spring.

A group of **Broad-winged Hawks** lifts off from the misty mountaintop trees of a Central American cloud forest where they have wintered. They flap and glide into the sunshine above the foggy forest and begin the long spring migration north.

A female **Great Horned Owl** in an Illinois woodlot discovers an abandoned Red-tailed Hawk nest high in a tree. She lines the nest with soft feathers from her breast and lays two large white eggs.

A female **American Kestrel** sits on her five eggs in the nesting box. Her mate calls to her, and the two birds fly toward each other. As they hover together, she takes food from him and flies home to the nest.

A pair of **Broad-winged Hawks** spend weeks building their nest of sticks in the fork of a tall forest tree. Finally the nest is lined with down, flowers, and grass, and the female lays three bluish white eggs.

The **Great Horned Owl** nest is home to two fluffy baby owls. One of the parents brings food for the hungry owlets, who devour their dinner in moments. The other parent spots a Red-tailed Hawk nearby and aggressively chases it away.

American Kestrels are learning to fly and hunt on their own. The eldest fledgling is the best hunter and captures a juicy grasshopper while his brothers and sisters watch from a perch near the nesting box.

The juvenile **Broad-winged Hawks** are nearly as large as their parents. The young birds like to perch on the branches of water-side trees and seem so tame that they allow humans to come within a few feet of them.

The young **owls** hunt on their own. One of the birds is perched in a tree at dusk when a curious human approaches. The bird lowers its head and fluffs its feathers in a defensive display meant to scare predators. The human backs off.

The days are short, and all the **Broad-winged Hawks** gather in great flocks. The birds fly high in the sky on warm thermals of air, soaring in wide circles, then turn away from their summer homes and begin the long flight back to the cloud forests of Central America.

Some of the young **Kestrels** fly south for the winter, but the eldest stays behind. As the first snowflakes fall it spies a field mouse nibbling on some grass seeds. In a flash the Kestrel appears above the mouse, hovers for a moment, then drops onto its meal.

The migrating birds have gone and at twilight it is so quiet the woods seem empty. Then the song of a **Great Horned Owl** booms through the half-light. A human child answers back and waits for the reply.

Why feathers?
Feathers (as on this Barred Owl) have many purposes: to keep birds warm, to help them fly, to provide camouflage, and to help direct sound to the ear openings.

FIVE

The Night Shift

After sunset, as twilight deepens into darkness, an exciting change takes place in forests and fields. The raptors that have been active during the day return to their roosts to sleep. At the same time other raptors, the owls, wake up and prepare to begin their day.

Owls have special tools to fly and hunt in the dark, and you will need special tools to find and watch them and listen to their haunting calls. The first tool you need is knowledge about these mysterious birds.

Night-time Differences

Owls and diurnal (active during the day) raptors have many things in common. Both are specialized predators with hooked beaks, grasping feet with talons, and fantastic eyesight. There are important differences, though, between diurnal raptors and owls. Here are some:

• Owls are mostly nocturnal (active at night) and have eyes that see well in near-total darkness, while the eyes of diurnal raptors have evolved to see well in daylight.

• Owls have longer and sharper talons than most other raptors, to pierce the bodies of prey more easily.

• Owls' hearing is much more sensitive than that of other raptors, and they have other unique tools and talents (called **adaptations**) as well.

Quiet flight
Owls, like this Saw-whet Owl, make almost no sound when they fly.

Are Owls Wiser than Other Birds?

Owls are known in folklore for their wisdom, probably because of their large heads and flat faces. In fact, their heads are large not to hold large brains but to hold large eyes, and their faces are disk-shaped to channel sound.

Eyeshine

Like domestic cats, many owls have a feature in their eyes called a **tapetum**, which makes them superb nocturnal predators. This mirror-like layer at the back of the retina reflects light (shines in the dark) and makes it easier for the owls to see.

Tools for Night Work

In addition to the tools they share with other raptors, owls have four special features that allow them to roam and hunt in the night: light-sensitive eyes, a dish-shaped face, unique ears, and silent flight.

Night Vision

Among animals whose eyes can pierce the darkness, an owl has few equals. The eyes of owls are very large for the size of the animal, almost as big as human eyes, and they take up more room in the bird's skull than its brain does. The larger the eye, the more light can enter the pupil, which is very important when you want to see in the dark. Owl eyes also have huge numbers of light-

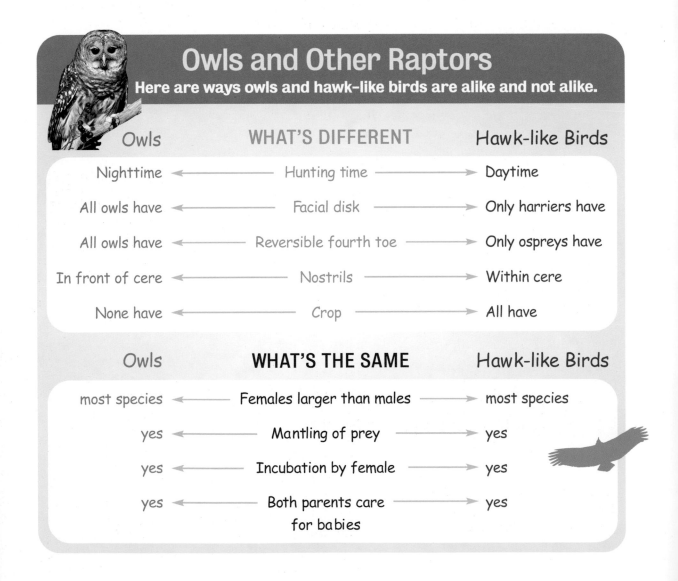

Owls and Other Raptors
Here are ways owls and hawk-like birds are alike and not alike.

Owls	WHAT'S DIFFERENT	Hawk-like Birds
Nighttime	Hunting time	Daytime
All owls have	Facial disk	Only harriers have
All owls have	Reversible fourth toe	Only ospreys have
In front of cere	Nostrils	Within cere
None have	Crop	All have

Owls	WHAT'S THE SAME	Hawk-like Birds
most species	Females larger than males	most species
yes	Mantling of prey	yes
yes	Incubation by female	yes
yes	Both parents care for babies	yes

sensitive cells (**rods**), many more than humans do, which help the birds see in very low light.

Honing in

The sense of hearing is as important to owls as the sense of sight is to diurnal raptors. The ear openings of many owls are large and **assymetrical,** meaning that one ear opening is often a different shape or size or at a different position compared to the other. A covering of soft feathers lies over the opening and helps funnel sound into the ear. One ear is placed higher on the owl's head than the other, allowing the bird to locate prey by the way the ears receive sounds from different points.

Facial Shape

One of the identifying features of an owl is its flat face, described as a **facial disk.** The flat dish shape of an owl's face gives these birds a wise and cuddly look. The reason for this shape has nothing to do with being smart or friendly, however; instead it helps the bird hear better. The feathers of the face are arranged so that they can collect and send sound waves toward the ears, helping the owl identify the location of the sounds it hears.

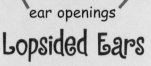

ear openings

Lopsided Ears

Owls' lopsided ears make it easy for them to figure out where a sound is coming from. When an owl hears the rustling of a tiny animal it tilts its head in order to pinpoint the creature's exact location.

Face it
The disk-shaped faces of the Barred Owl (above) and the Barn Owl (right) direct sound waves toward the ears.

Owl feathers

Owl flight is silent because of the feather structure. Notice the serrated edge – this muffles the sound and makes the bird's flight silent.

owl feather's serrated edge

On Silent Wings

Most owls make no sound when they fly. An owl's quiet flight is thanks to its feathers. While the feathers of most birds are smooth and glossy, owl feathers have a soft fluffy front edge. A smooth glossy falcon feather is very aerodynamic, but as the air slips over the feather's edge it makes noise. An owl feather creates more drag, making it harder to fly, but air passing over it makes almost no sound at all. Owls don't need to be super-fast like falcons because they catch their prey by surprise. But to hunt by surprise you must be silent.

How to Find Owls

You can find owls in just about every habitat, from tropical forest to arctic tundra. Why not start looking for the owl most likely to be living near you? Check at right to locate your local owls.

Barn Owl

Lives in farm buildings, open fields, along rivers bordering open meadows or fields, suburbs, towns, and deserts. (See p.42 for more information.)

Barred Owl

Lives in groves of evergreen trees. If disturbed will fly only a few yards to another tree. (See p.46 for more information.)

Camouflage
The feathers of this Barn Owl are unevenly colored, helping him remain hidden from his prey.

Northern Saw-whet Owl

Lives in dark stands of conifers or thick mixed forests. Roosts in dense evergreen thickets on winter days. (See p.53 for more information.)

Eastern & Western Screech-owls

Live in evergreen, mixed, and deciduous forests and along forest edges. In winter they sun themselves by poking their heads out of tree holes. (See pp 49–50 for more information.)

Great Horned Owl

Lives in many different types of habitat such as forests, woodlands, along rivers, open fields, and meadows, farmland, and suburbs. (See p.45 for more information.)

Going Owling

Owls are creatures of habit and keep visiting the same places over and over. The perches an owl visits regularly to sleep, eat, or just relax, like a couple of comfortable branches in a tall tree, are called **roosts.** Find an active roost, and there's a good chance an owl is there or will be before too long.

Clues: Pellets and Whitewash

Looking for what owls leave behind after they digest their meals can help you find the owls themselves and also teach you a lot about them.

Whitewash is the polite name for white paint-like splashes of owl poop that cover branches, the base of a tree, and the forest floor beneath a roost.

Owl pellets are small, sausage-shaped pellets owls cough up, containing the undigested fur, feathers, and bone of its prey. If you find these on the ground you are probably near or under a roost. See pages 98–99 to learn how to dissect an owl pellet and find out what one bird has been eating.

Finding a Roost

An owl will rest in a roost tree during the day. To locate the owl look very carefully at nearby branches, especially where the branch connects to the trunk of the tree. The mottled brown and white coloring of most owls is excellent camouflage so the birds are often hard to see. Look for a lump that looks out of place and then use binoculars to get a better look. And be very quiet so you don't frighten an owl that might be there.

If you discover a roost at night, shine your flashlight into the branches of the tree directly above the whitewash. If you see the owl remember that the bright beam of a flashlight can disturb these birds. Don't shine the light directly into the bird's eyes. Watch it for a few seconds, then turn off the light and walk away quietly.

Best conditions
Owls are most active on clear, moonlit nights without wind.

Whole **owl pellet** at actual size.

Talking Back to Owls

If you hear owls at night you can have a wonderful adventure by going out and calling to them. Great Horned Owls and Barred Owls may answer you and even fly to where you are. But be sure not to do it for more than about 10 minutes or you might bother the owl.

Some people play tape recordings of owl calls rather than trying to imitate them. This is often discouraged, for there is some evidence that recordings may bother the birds and can even cause them to abandon territories. Some very territorial owls, like the Northern Saw-whet, might even attack the recorder. Imitating owls is more fun than playing a tape, and when the owl returns your call you know that bird is talking to you.

Go on an Owl Prowl

The best times to search for owls are during calm nights with clear or mostly clear skies and some moonlight. The moon provides light so you can see better, and the lack of wind makes it easier to hear and locate calling owls. The temperature is not important. Owls are most active during the beginning of mating season. In most of North America this occurs in springtime, while in tropical regions this happens at the end of the dry season.

When getting ready for an owling expedition, be sure to have an adult with you, anddress for the weather. Leave the tape player at home and try to attract the birds by imitating their calls.

Keep your ears and eyes open, and HAPPY OWLING!

Learn to Speak "Owl"

The best way to learn to talk with an owl is to imitate the call you hear at night. Here are some commonly heard voices:

Great Horned Owl. "Hoo hoo-hoo, hoo, hoo!" (sounds like "Who's awake? Me, too!")

Barred Owl. "Hoo-hoo hoo-hoo, hoo-hoo hoo-hoo-ahh" (sounds like "Who cooks for you? Who cooks for you all?")

Eastern Screech-owl. A whinny or wail, rising and falling in pitch.

SIX

Raptor Aid

Through much of history, raptors and people have not gotten along very well. People didn't understand raptors, so they didn't see how valuable they are to a healthy environment. This lack of understanding led to the needless killing of thousands and thousands of birds over many decades and across the continent. Some were shot or poisoned. Others died when their habitat was destroyed or when poachers stole eggs or young from their nests. Today we know more about these magnificent birds and much of the killing has stopped, but not all. There is still much to do before raptors are better understood.

For many years hawks and other raptors were considered a major threat to farming and ranching and to smaller birds. This mistaken idea led people to shoot thousands of raptors. In many areas around the country this killing became a cruel sport. At Hawk Mountain in Pennsylvania, a ridge famous for the large numbers of

Largest Living Raptor

The largest raptor alive in North America today is the rare California Condor, with a wingspan ranging from 9 to 11 feet (2.8 to 3.4 m) across. The birds stand about 4 feet (1.2 m) tall and are cloaked with dark feathers. The naked head pokes out of a collar of feathers, making the bird look as if it is wearing a turtleneck sweater.

Hawks aloft
Thousands of people visit Hawk Mountain, Pennsylvania, every year to watch the spectacular hawk migration.

raptors that pass during migration, gunmen once shot thousands of birds each year for target practice. In 1934 Hawk Mountain became the world's first sanctuary where raptors are protected and visitors (and scientists) can watch their amazing migrations.

Pesticides are chemicals designed to kill insects and other pests. Unfortunately, some pesticides also hurt or kill other animals such as raptors. One such pesticide, DDT, nearly wiped out Bald Eagles, Ospreys, Peregrine Falcons, and other birds of prey in some parts of North America by causing a thinning of the shell of the birds' eggs. DDT is now banned in many countries, but is still used in others where some raptors spend the winter. Many other pesticides known to harm raptors are still being used throughout North America and other parts of the world. Fortunately, scientists and educators are working to end these and other threats to our wild neighbors.

Eye on the sky
At Cape May, New Jersey, naturalists and visitors monitor the thousands of birds that pass every fall on their journey south.

Keeping Track

Strike up the band
Bird bands (above) are an important way of tracking raptors, such as this Northern Saw-whet Owl (below left) and Sharp-shinned Hawk (right). Banded birds also teach scientists about longevity and travel patterns.

Keeping track of birds that can fly almost as fast as an airplane and travel thousands of miles during each migration is pretty tough. But tracking raptors is very important so people can learn more about them and help them survive and thrive. Information learned through tracking raptors includes where a certain species can be found, especially where it lives in summer and winter, as well as how much time it spends in each place during migration. The most common ways used to track raptors are banding, radar, and satellite telemetry (using satellites to pick up signals). Check out Resources for Web sites that track individual raptors.

Banding Birds

A bird band is an aluminum strip that is attached to the leg of a bird. Each band has its own special number that gives each bird its own identity.

Helping a licensed bird bander to band raptors is exciting. The birds are attracted to a special trap that tangles up their feet. They are then carefully placed in holding containers until they are ready for banding. A band of the right size is attached around the bird's leg, without

radio receivers

harming the bird. Once the band is in place the bird is measured and weighed and its sex and age are recorded. The most fun is watching the bird fly away when released. Ask your local nature center if there are raptor banding demonstrations in your area.

Birds on Weather Radar

The faint echoes of flying birds on a radar screen were first observed shortly after radar was invented. The echoes were just a curiosity until the 1990s, when a new type of radar, called NEXRAD (next generation radar), was developed and became a tool to study and help birds. NEXRAD gives a very clear 3-D view of the area it is studying. It is most often used to track the course and strength of storms, but it can also track flocks of migrating birds, both at night and during the day.

The Eye in the Sky

Radio tags are tracking tools that can be attached to wildlife. Scientists can observe the radio signal the tag emits and locate the animal's position. As the animal moves, scientists have a record of where it goes. Radio tags were once so big and heavy that for years they were used only on large animals like bears and whales. They were also limited by the short life of their batteries. In recent years, lightweight solar-powered devices have been used to study the migration and feeding patterns of Bald Eagles and other large raptors. These tags send out signals that are picked up by orbiting satellites and relayed through a global positioning system (GPS) to provide the bird's exact location.

California Condors

The rarest raptor in North America is the California Condor. In the 1980s the last 25 or so remaining condors were captured and brought to a special captive living area, where scientists hoped they would breed. By 1998 there were 150 California Condors. By mid-2001, there were 184 California Condors.

Many of those birds have been released in the wild since then, with 34 flying over central and southern California and an additional 22 in Arizona. Some of these now carry radio tags, as shown in photographs above.

How to help a
raptor that looks
injured

If you find a raptor
that is acting
strangely, the first
thing to do is find out
if it is really hurt.
Some raptors, such as
young birds and some
owls, can seem very
tame. A bird that sits
quietly but follows
your movements with
its eyes is probably
not injured. Young
birds on the ground
that look fine should
be left alone because
the parents are usu-
ally nearby and still
caring for them.

Raptor Rehab

The natural world is a tough place to live. Making a mis-
take can be fatal, and getting a second chance doesn't
happen very often. The aim of raptor rehabilitation is to
give raptors that have bumped into some bad luck a second chance at survival. If left in the wild, these injured
birds would probably die. But given medicine, care, and
time to heal, many of those same birds can survive to
once again take their place in the sky.

Please Release Me

The type of treatment a bird gets at a rehab center
depends on what types of injuries it has and how serious
they are. Many injuries happen when raptors are hit by
cars and trucks, or when they fly into windows, electrical
towers, and power lines. Some birds recover and can be
released in just a few weeks, while others may need treatment for a year or two.

After they recover some raptors, like Bald Eagles, can be released at any time of year, as long as there is some open water where they can catch fish. Other raptors, such as many hawks, are let go during the warmer months when the right food is available.

Sometimes an injury is so bad that the bird will never recover enough to survive in the wild. These otherwise healthy raptors are used in teaching programs across the continent. The programs are designed to allow people to be exposed to and learn about these powerful and beautiful animals up close, a treat few people ever have.

Getting Involved

Raptor rehabilitation centers are great places to volunteer. Jobs you can do range from keeping the facilities neat and clean to exercising the recovering birds. Other tasks include working with the resident education raptors (the ones too badly injured to return to the wild) and transporting injured raptors to the center. Whatever your job, you will have the opportunity to see raptors up close and personal while helping them.

Raptors are powerful, majestic, and essential in our environment. You could spend your life studying them!

Raptor 911

The Southeastern Raptor Rehabilitation Center at Auburn University recommends following these guidelines when handling or moving an injured raptor.

✚ Don't feed the bird.
✚ Handle the bird as little as possible, wear thick gloves, and cover the bird with a towel.
✚ Put the raptor in a covered cardboard box (with air holes) that is a little bigger than the bird.
✚ Keep the box covered and in a dark, warm place.
✚ Injured raptors can be dangerous. Be alert!
✚ Bring the raptor to a licensed raptor rehabilitator.

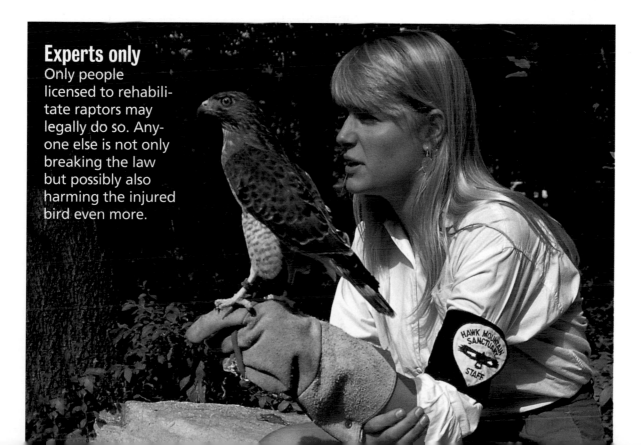

Experts only
Only people licensed to rehabilitate raptors may legally do so. Anyone else is not only breaking the law but possibly also harming the injured bird even more.

Human help
A hacking box can shelter baby raptors until they can survive on their own.

Hacking

When the population of a raptor species falls to very low numbers, so low that its survival may be in doubt, scientists use a method called **hacking**, hoping slowly to boost the birds' numbers.

Hacking involves raising some of the threatened birds in captivity, such as a zoo. Scientists take the wild birds' eggs and incubate and hatch them in a laboratory. After a while the baby raptors are brought to a release site and raised in a big box. This box gives the young birds a view of their new surroundings and lets them slowly get used to their new home, so that when they are let go they will stay nearby to live and raise their own families someday.

Hacking has helped increase the numbers of many raptors all over the continent and allowed them to return to their homes in the wild. Some of the most successful hacking programs involve Peregrine Falcons and Bald Eagles (see pages 92–93).

Our Three Most Endangered Raptors

California Condor

Spotted Owl

Snail Kite

The main way birds become endangered is through loss of their habitat. Snail Kites' population shrank when Florida's freshwater marshes were drained. Spotted Owls suffer from the cutting of old-growth forests. Condors have an additional problem: They were shot because they were considered a threat to livestock. All three of these species are slowly beginning to come back.

Habitat Is Home

Habitat is home, and no living thing lives alone. The web of life links all creatures and all habitats. When even a small amount of a habitat is damaged, it affects animals and plants both near and far and in many different places. When less than a quarter of a forest is cut down the water in the streams becomes dirtier, some creatures begin to die, and others move away. The change in the forest can then affect the habitat that borders the forest, such as when dirty forest streams flow into a marsh. The change in the marsh affects another nearby habitat and so on. It is much easier to protect a healthy habitat than to fix a damaged one.

Into the Wild

Many raptor rehabilitation centers have "adopt a raptor" programs. Some rehab centers offer a chance for people to release rehabilitated raptors back to the wild. For a set donation you can hold and release a raptor, then watch as it climbs into the sky. People that have released raptors say it is a spine-tingling experience like no other they have ever had.

Protecting Habitat

Many people know that by protecting habitat we not only help wildlife, but we make the world a better place for people as well. Remember that animals don't live alone but in communities of many different creatures. By protecting the habitat of raptors we protect the homes of dozens of other species, from fish and frogs to mice and songbirds.

There are many organizations that are working to conserve habitats. These groups often buy large pieces of land where they set up and run sanctuaries for wildlife along with educational programs, wildlife rehabilitation centers, and other programs to conserve the environment. Local, state/provincial, and federal governments also protect habitat by setting up parks or preserves and passing laws to protect wildlife and the environment. A good way to help protect habitat is to join and work with the conservation organizations near you.

owl feather   hawk feather

Flying free
A Peregrine Falcon swoops for a snack.

Restoring Raptors

There are two main reasons why raptors decline or even become extinct: through natural causes or because of people's actions. There are also two ways raptors are returned to an environment: through natural causes or because of people's help. Living things have been adapting to new environments for a few hundred million years, but sometimes humans change the environment so quickly animals can not adapt fast enough. And so they need a little help from us. Many people are now working hard to reintroduce and save raptors. The biggest successes so far are the return of the Peregrine Falcon and Bald Eagle.

Falcons Fly Again

Peregrine Falcons are among the fastest animals on earth, but their amazing speed hasn't helped them avoid pesticides, pollution, and habitat loss. So many of these birds died in the 1950s and 1960s that Peregrines were placed on the endangered species list.

The first hacking programs didn't do well because many young birds were killed by Great Horned Owls. Scientists then moved the programs to cities like New York, Boston, Baltimore, and Chicago, where there was a good supply of pigeons but no Great Horned Owls.

Today Peregrine Falcons live in many cities. Hacking programs in rural and wilderness areas have allowed Peregrines to return to places as different as Acadia National Park in Maine and the Bow River in Alberta.

Habitat Loss

The habitat of the Snail Kite is the Florida freshwater marshes (Everglades) where its prey, the apple snail, lives. Because the Snail Kite eats only apple snails, it can't survive anywhere else in North America. If the habitat of the Snail Kite and the apple snails it feeds on is changed by draining or pollution of the marsh, the snails will disappear and the kites with them.

The Eagle Has Landed

A few decades ago, so many Bald Eagles were killed by pesticides and illegal hunting that this symbol of the United States was listed as an endangered species. Many restoration and reintroduction programs were started and have been so successful that this majestic raptor has returned to places where it hadn't been seen in years.

An example of a successful eagle hacking program is in central California. The Ventana Wilderness Society raised and released 66 birds in less than 20 years. Today Bald Eagles are again soaring over the cliff edge of Big Sur and other areas of the central California coast.

Condors Rebounding

The California Condor is the largest raptor in North America but was so close to extinction that in the 1980s only a couple of dozen remained in the wild. Habitat loss, poisoning, and shooting were some of the many reasons why condors almost disappeared. Scientists captured the birds and began a program to save this huge raptor. The program fertilized eggs in the laboratory and then raised and released birds into carefully chosen habitats in California and Arizona.

Progress is slow but the birds are making a comeback. On June 1, 2001, the total number of California Condors had grown to 184, with 55 of the birds wild and free.

Good News

Although Bald Eagles are still listed as threatened in Canada, in the United States their status has recently been changed to "sensitive," which shows how much their populations have grown. They are much more common than they were in the 1970s.

Letting go

It is a thrilling experience to release a raptor into the wild. This boy is holding a juvenile Red-tailed Hawk.

Raptor Conservation Projects

Osprey ▲
Communities building nesting platforms; satellite tracking projects underway

Swallow-tailed Kite ▶
Satellite and radio tracking programs

Northern Harrier ● ↘
Protection of habitat with help from ranchers and farmers

Golden Eagle ▲
Hacking programs; platforms added to utility poles to protect eagles from being electrocuted

Bald Eagle ▶ ▲
Hacking of eggs and young, especially in the East, in effort to reestablish populations has been widespread and successful

Harris's Hawk ▶ ↘
Reintroduced in southern California; insulating utility poles and adding perching arms to reduce electrocution

Broad-winged Hawk ●
Tracking of birds with satellite transmitters

Red-shouldered Hawk ● ↘
Protecting large blocks of forest and wetlands with help of private land owners

Red-tailed Hawk ● ▲
Utility poles outfitted with platforms to keep these and other raptors from being electrocuted

Swainson's Hawk ●
Efforts to stop use of insecticides that have killed many Swainson's Hawks on their wintering range

Ferruginous Hawk ▶ ↘
Protection of native grasslands, building and placing nesting platforms

American Kestrel ● ↘
Building and putting up kestrel nest boxes in many areas; leaving large, dead trees standing

Endangered Ratings:

● common   ◗ uncommon
■ edge of endangered   ★ rare
▲ increasing   ➡ decreasing   ◆ stable

Prairie Falcon ● ◗ ➡

Human-made cavities and nesting platforms on cliffs

Peregrine Falcon ◗ ■

Re-introduced into former range by captive breeding and hacking, also in cities by putting nest platforms on tall buildings and bridges

Barn Owl ◗ ★

Nest box projects in some states and captive breeding and release efforts and re-introductions in others

Great Horned Owl ●

None; this predator is sometimes removed by wildlife managers from certain areas when it preys on endangered species

Barred Owl ● ▲

Putting up nest boxes

Spotted Owl ■

Major efforts to protect old-growth forest habitat in Pacific Northwest

Eastern Screech-owl ● ➡

Putting up nest boxes

Western Screech-owl ●

Building and putting up nest boxes

Elf Owl ● ■

Reintroduced in California; has used nest boxes in West Texas

Northern Saw-whet Owl ◗

Building and putting up nest boxes; effort to preserve wood-lots in Alberta

Burrowing Owl ● ➡

Re-introductions since 1985 in Minnesota, Iowa, and South Dakota; will use artificial nest tunnels.

Short-eared Owl ● ➡

Burning stubble fields before April 1 can help with habitat needs

SEVEN

Cool Raptor Projects to Make & Do

magnified pellet and
partly dissected pellet

Dissect an Owl Pellet

Adult owls, unlike diurnal raptors, usually swallow their prey whole.
The bird's stomach acids turn the meat into liquid, while the bones
and fur form a pellet that is coughed up and spit out. Pull apart a pellet, identify the skulls and beaks and so on, and you'll know what that
owl ate, often right down to the species of mouse and how many
were eaten (count the skulls). If an owl makes two pellets a day, how
many mice, shrews, or birds must it catch in a week, month, or year?

Owl pellets can be from less than 1 inch (2.5 cm) to more than
4 inches (10 cm) long and contain dozens of clues about the prey
that became that owl's meal. Before dissecting (taking apart) the
pellet, measure it and note its shape. (You can even trace it or draw
it.) This may give you an idea about what owl made the pellet. Look
in an animal tracking book for pictures to help identify your pellet.

To pick apart an owl pellet, follow these steps.

1. Wear gloves. Place the pellet on a paper towel. Use tweezers and a hand lens to help you look for and re-move skulls, jawbones, teeth, and beaks.

2. With the tweezers place the skulls, jaw bones, teeth, and beaks in a row.

3. With the help of a field guide, try to reassemble the skele-ton of a tiny animal.

4. When you have fin-ished your dissection, you can dispose of your pellet in the trash or recycle its contents into the soil of a local forest.

Clues

Examine the contents of the pellet — skulls, bones, teeth, feathers, etc. — for clues about what animals became dinner for this owl.

? Is the pellet made up mostly of insects? It was probably made by a Screech-owl.

? Is a skull broken? It's probably a bird's. Is it whole? It's proba-bly a rodent's.

? Do the teeth have red tips? They proba-bly belonged to a shrew, which eats meat, not seeds.

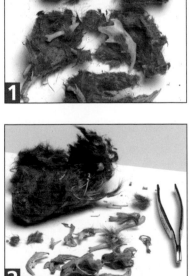

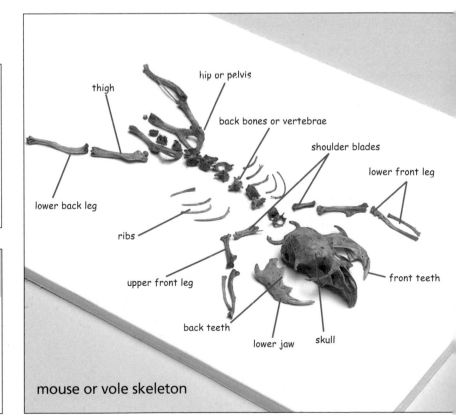

thigh

hip or pelvis

back bones or vertebrae

shoulder blades

lower front leg

lower back leg

ribs

upper front leg

front teeth

back teeth

lower jaw

skull

mouse or vole skeleton

Build a Raptor Nestbox

This nestbox will house an American Kestrel, a Northern Saw-whet Owl, or a Screech-owl. The only difference among boxes for these birds is the size of the entrance hole.

The entrance hole will decide which raptor will come to the nestbox. The box shown below has a 3-inch-diameter (7.6 cm) entrance hole, which is right for American Kestrels. The Northern Saw-whet Owl requires only a 2½-inch-diameter (6.4 cm) hole; the Screech-owl a 2¾-inch (7 cm) hole.

> **Note:** An adult should help with cutting and preparation of this project.

You will need:

Wood
- ⅞" x 9¾" x 8' (2.2 cm x 24.8 cm x 2.4 m) rough-cut cedar board
- ½" (1.3 cm) maple dowel (optional)

Screws and nails
- Twenty-six 1⅝" (4 cm) long drywall screws
- Two galvanized 6d, 2" (5.1 cm) finishing nails
- One brass or galvanized #6 x 1½" (3.8 cm) flat-head wood screw
- One brass or galvanized #6 x 2" (5.1 cm) pan-head wood screw, with washer to fit
- Heavy-duty staples

Power and hand tools
- Table saw or carpenter's handsaw and miter box
- Keyhole saw or expansion bit (for cutting entrance hole)
- Power or hand drill
- Drill bits: ³⁄₁₆" (.469 cm), ⅛" (.313 cm), ¼" (.625 cm), and ⅜" (.938 cm)
- Claw hammer
- Phillips-head screwdriver, or power drill fitted with screwdriver bits
- Carpenter's square
- Tape measure or yard (meter) stick
- Pencil
- Rasp or awl (optional)
- Staple gun
- Sandpaper (optional)

Side opens for monitoring and cleaning

For the Adult: Cutting and Preparation

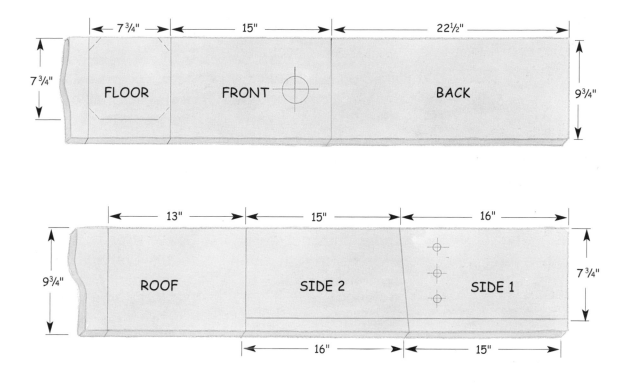

1. Cut out all pieces of wood, using dimensions above, and predrill nail holes.

2. Cut the entrance hole with the keyhole saw. The bottom of the hole should be located 9–10" (22.9–25.4 cm) above the floor.

3. For kestrels, cut an inside perch from one half of the entrance hole wood. Screw this 3" (7.6 cm) below the bottom of the entrance hole. (Do not use for owls.)

4. Cut ⅝" (1.6 cm) off each of the four corners of the floor to create drainage holes. Or, drill four or five ¼" (.6 cm) drainage holes in the floor. Drill three ⅜" (1 cm) holes near the top of the nonpivoting side for ventilation.

Tip: The back edge of the roof and the top edge of the front will fit better if you bevel-cut them at 5 degrees. Or you can nail or screw a ½" (1.3 cm) maple dowel where the roof and back meet to keep rain from seeping in.

For Kids and Adults: Assembly

1. Screw or nail side 1 to the back of the box, rough side in.

2. Make sure that the hardware cloth strip and inside perch (the latter only for kestrels) have been fastened below the entrance hole. Then screw or nail the front to side 1.

3. Screw or nail the floor to the back and side 1, recessing it ¼" (.6 cm) from the bottom.

inside view of *front*

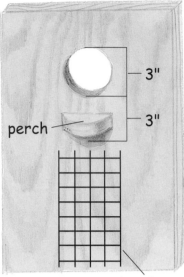

perch

3"

3"

hardware cloth

4. Now attach side 2, using two pivot nails near the top. Note that the pivot nails must be lined up exactly opposite each other, and that this side is ¼" (.6 cm) shorter than the other, to allow it to swing open properly. Predrill a centered ⅛" (.313 cm) guide hole, then use the pan-head screw and a washer to fasten the bottom of this side to the floor.

5. Screw or nail on the roof to all sides.

6. If you have not bevel-cut the back edge of the top, nail or screw the ½" (1.3 cm) dowel where the roof meets the back.

Setting Up the Box

For kestrels, mount the box at least 10 feet (3.1 m) high, and preferably 12 to 20 feet (3.7–6.1 m) up, in open

Inside the box

If you use finished lumber, staple or nail a 3" x 6" (7.6 cm x 15.2 cm) piece of ¼" (.625 cm) galvanized wire mesh (hardware cloth) to the inside of the front, below the inside perch to enable the young to climb to the entrance; be sure to bend sharp edges away. Alternatively, you can rout or score the front inside with a sharp tool such as a rasp or awl to provide a grip for the young.

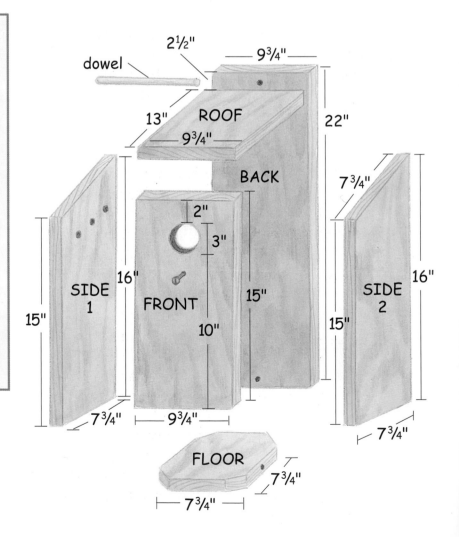

country — farmland, a meadow, or an abandoned field. Locate the box 15 to 30 feet (4.6–9.2 m) from a snag, or a tree with dead limbs. Males use such branches as prey "plucking posts." Face the box away from prevailing storms, usually south or east. Space boxes about 1 mile (1.6 km) apart, and no closer than ½ mile (.8 km). Kestrels require a minimum of 1 acre (.4 ha) per pair.

Screech-owls generally prefer open woodland. Place the box 15–50 feet (4.6–15.4 m) up in a tree in the woods. Place on a straight trunk that is wider than the nestbox. Boxes should be 100 feet (30.5 m) apart. Make sure that there is an unobstructed flying area nearby.

Northern Saw-whet Owls also tend to nest rather high, so mount the box 14 feet (4.3 m) off the ground, or higher in deciduous, evergreen, or mixed forests, woodlots, and swamps. Place the box in a mature, live tree, preferably near water.

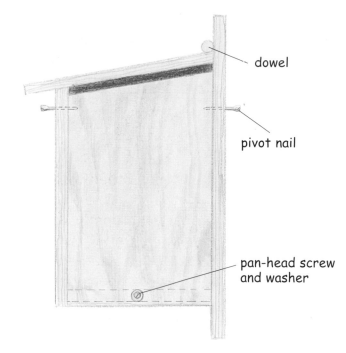

dowel

pivot nail

pan-head screw and washer

Mounting

Attach boxes to metal or wooden poles or large dead trees (of sound wood) with bolts or lag screws. Be sure to wrap a 30-inch-wide (76 cm) sleeve of aluminum around wooden poles or dead trees, to prevent predators from reaching the nestbox. Boxes can also be placed on silos, barns, windmills, or even on the backs of highway signs (be sure to obtain permission from the proper agency first).

Place only 1 inch (2.5 cm) of wood shavings (not cedar) in the bottom of the box as nesting material for kestrels; 2 to 3 inches (5.1–7.6 cm) for screech-owls and Northern Saw-whet Owls. Do not use sawdust, because it may irritate the nostrils and eyes of the nestlings.

Painting/Staining

You do not need to paint cedar boxes. Pine boxes will last longer if you do, but untreated pine boxes may last approximately 10 years. Be sure to use light-colored exterior latex house paint, and treat only the outside. For owls, boxes can be painted or stained dark brown on the outside only. Do not use paints or stains that contain lead or toxic wood preservatives.

Make a Raptor Mobile

You will need:

glue stick or diluted white glue

oak tag (or manila file folders), black poster-board, or cardboard

scissors

large paper clip

thread or monofilament

black paint, or paint colors or markers to mimic the colors of the real bird

Raptor silhouettes can make a beautiful mobile to float over your bed, or you can hang them individually around your room. You'll soon be an expert at identifying raptors by their shapes!

The bird shapes on the right hand page are drawn at the correct proportion to each other. Their relative size is one of the clues you can use to identify them.

What to do:

1. Photocopy the facing page. Enlarge by 200% or more if you wish.

2. Cut out the bird shapes, glue them on the oak tag, poster-board, or cardboard and then cut them out. Write the bird's species on the back of the shape.

3. Poke two small holes in the bird shape with a paper clip. Thread the monofilament or thread through the holes and tie in a double knot.

4. Hang your raptor silhouettes from a branch or individually around your room.

Swallow-
tailed Kite

Osprey

Golden Eagle

Great
Horned
Owl

Northern Harrier

Crested Caracara

Rough-legged Hawk
(Buteo)

Peregrine Falcon

Barn Owl

Cooper's
Hawk

Turkey Vulture

Journal Keeping

Keeping a record of your observations is important. Think of Charles Darwin and his journey aboard the *H. M. S. Beagle*. Without a journal, he would have had a hard time remembering all the amazing things he saw and might not have written his famous work *On The Origin of Species*.

What goes into a journal? Everyone has his or her own way of recording observations. The most important thing is to write clearly and completely so you can understand what you have written a week, a month, or many years later.

Sketches are helpful. A picture can show or tell you things that words sometimes just cannot. Since pencil smudges over time and can be difficult to read, it's best to use a pen with permanent ink.

What should be recorded in a journal?

Date: The exact date is absolutely important.
Time: Record the time when you start your observations and the time when you end.
Weather: Record the temperature (or write "hot," "warm," or "cool"); wind conditions including direction; the type of clouds or how much of the sky is covered with clouds (10%, 50%). Weather details are important because as you become a good hawk watcher, you'll

notice weather-related patterns in hawk migration.

Location: Be specific. For example, 1.4 miles (2.3km) north of the intersection of Routes 8 and 20, on the right-hand side of the road.

Description: Write everything down no matter how inconsequential you think it is now. Drawings will help explain what you are seeing. Take notes as things happen. Try to identify the prey the raptor is carrying or eating.

Finally, don't forget to put your name, address, and phone number on the inside cover of your book. If for some reason it is lost, the finder will have a way to return it. Laminating the cover or putting the journal in a plastic bag is also a good idea. This not only keeps it clean but also protects it from weather conditions such as dew, frost, and humidity.

Make photocopies of the following page and use them to record information about the raptors you see.

What I Saw and Where I Saw It

Date: _____ Time: _____

Weather:

Temperature:_____ Is it calm?_____

Windy?_____ Wind direction_____

What types of clouds are in the sky? _____

What percent of the sky is covered with clouds? _____

Location: _____

Description of bird: _____

_____

_____

_____

Behavior of bird: _____

_____

_____

Other notes: _____

_____

_____

_____

_____

Use this space to draw your bird.

What I Saw and Where I Saw It

Date: _____ Time: _____

Weather:

Temperature:_____ Is it calm?_____

Windy?_____ Wind direction_____

What types of clouds are in the sky? _____

What percent of the sky is covered with clouds? _____

Location: _____

Description of bird: _____

_____

_____

_____

Behavior of bird:_____

_____

_____

Other notes:_____

_____

_____

_____

_____

Use this space to draw your bird.

Match Parents With Their Offspring

Glossary

Accipiter. Type of hawk, usually with short wings and long tail, that preys on smaller birds it catches on the wing (examples: Sharp-shinned and Cooper's Hawks)

Aerie. A nest, usually made by a raptor, on a cliff or other high place

Bill. The beak of a bird

Binocular vision. Three-dimensional vision produced by overlap of vision from both eyes

Branching. When young raptors remain near nest on branches, exercising their wings for weeks before fledging

Brood. The baby birds that hatch from a clutch of eggs

Buteo. A type of hawk, usually with broad wings and short tail, that soars and often preys on rodents (examples: Red-tailed, Swainson's, and Ferruginous Hawks)

Carrion. A dead animal or rotting flesh used as food by some animals such as vultures

Cere. A fleshy featherless area around the nostrils of many raptors

Clutch. The number of eggs laid by a female bird in one nesting period

Cones. Cells in the eye that work best in strong light and are used to see colors and form sharp images

Crest. Slightly longer feathers on the head or neck that when raised form a pointed tuft

Depth perception. The ability to see an object and at the same time determine how far away it is

Diurnal. Active during the day and asleep at night

Falconry. Breeding and training captive hawks, most often falcons, to hunt prey for sport

Falcon tooth. A notch in the upper part of the hooked beak of a falcon used to sever the spinal cord of prey

Field of view. All that can be seen at one time, as when looking through binoculars

Fledgling. A young bird that has left the nest

Glide. To fly downward without flapping wings

Hacking. Taking eggs from the wild and placing them in an incubator or in the nest of a related species for hatching. Young birds are then put in hacking boxes in the right habitat and later released. A way of reintroducing raptors into areas where they no longer breed

Hawking. Catching prey in flight

Mantling. Standing over a fresh kill with wings spread, to hide it from others

Mobbing. When potential prey harasses a predator to drive it away

Monocular vision. Vision resulting when only one eye is used to see an object, common in non-raptors with eyes on the sides of their heads

Nocturnal. Active at night and asleep during the day

Objective. The binocular lens closest to the object being viewed

Ocular. The eyepiece of binoculars

Passerine. Singing and perching birds of the order Passiformes with three forward-pointing toes and one backward-pointing toe

Predators. Animals that hunt other animals for food

Prey. Animals that are hunted and eaten by other animals

Primaries. Long feathers on the tip of a wing

Raptor. A bird of prey

Rods. Highly light-sensitive cells in the eye

Roost. To settle for rest or sleep; a place where birds rest or sleep

Sideburn. A dark vertical mark behind the eye, most often found on falcons

Soar. To fly, without flapping wings, usually in spirals on rising air

Stoop. A steep, fast dive through the air in pursuit of prey

Talon. The claw of a raptor

Tapetum. A membrane in the eye that reflects light

Thermal. A rising body of warm air

Trait. A feature used to tell different types of animals apart

Tubercle. A small round bump

Updraft. A wind going up over an obstacle

Resources

Selected Hawk Watching Sites in North America

Fall Sites

Arizona
*South Rim (Yaki Pt. & Lipan Pt.), Grand Canyon National Park
(early September–early November)

British Columbia
Beechy Head, East Sooke Park, Victoria, British Colombia
(mid-September– late October)

California
*Golden Gate-Marin Headlands/Hawk Hill, near San Francisco, California
(late August–late December)

Weldon, California Turkey Vulture Count
(September–mid-October)

Connecticut
*Quaker Ridge, Greenwich Audubon Center, Greenwich, Connecticut
(late-August–mid November)

Lighthouse Point State Park, New Haven, Connecticut
(late August–early November)

Florida
*Florida Keys, near Marathon, Florida — especially falcons
(mid-September–early November)

Idaho
Lucky Peak, near Boise, Idaho
(late August–early November)

Iowa
Hitchcock Nature Area, Honey Creek, Iowa
(September–mid-December)

Maine
Mount Agamenticus, York, Maine
(September–October)

Massachusetts
Mount Wachusett, Princeton, Massachusetts
(late August–early November)

Mount Watatic, Ashburnham, Massachusetts
(late August–early November)

Mount Tom, Easthampton, Massachusetts
(late August–early November)

Montana
*Bridger Bowl Ski Area, near Bozeman, Montana
(September–October)

Nevada
*Goshute Mountains, south of West Wendover, Nevada
(August–November)

New Hampshire
Pack Monadnock, Miller State Park, Peterborough, New Hampshire
(late August–early November)

New Jersey
*Cape May Point State Park, Cape May Point, New Jersey
(mid-August–mid-November)

Montclair Hawk Lookout Sanctuary, Montclair, New Jersey
(mid-August–mid-November)

New Mexico
*Manzano Mountains, south of Albuquerque, New Mexico
(late August–early November)

New York
Fire Island (Robert Moses State Park), Long Island, New York
(mid-September– mid-November)

Central Park (Belvedere Castle), Manhattan, New York
(mid-September best)

North Carolina
Mount Pisgah, Asheville, North Carolina
(September–October)

Ontario
*Holiday Beach Provincial Park, Amherstburg, Ontario
(late August–November)

Oregon
*Bonney Butte, Government Camp, Oregon
(September–October)

Pennsylvania
*Hawk Mountain Sanctuary, Kempton, Pennsylvania
(mid-August–mid-December)

indicates that this site has education programs and/or special events

Texas
Smith Point, Galveston
Bay, near Houston
(mid-August–mid-November)

*Hazel Bazemore County
Park, Corpus Christi, Texas
(mid-August–mid-November)
(largest raptor concentration in
U.S. and Canada)

Utah
Wellsville Mountains, Utah
(late August–late October)

Vermont
Putney Mountain,
Putney, Vermont
(late August–mid-November)

Virginia
*Kiptopeke State Park,
Kiptopeke, Virginia
(late August–late November)

Washington
*Chelan Ridge (Copper
Mountain), Chelan,
Washington
(late August–mid-October)

West Virginia
Hanging Rock Raptor
Observatory, Peter's
Mountain, West Virginia (late
August–late November)

Spring Sites
Michigan
*Whitefish Point, Paradise,
Michigan (mid-March–May)

New Jersey
Sandy Hook, Gateway
National Recreation
Center, New Jersey
(second half of April)

New Mexico
*Sandia Mountains,
Albuquerque, New Mexico
(late February–early May)

New York
*Braddock Bay Park,
near Rochester, New York
(early March–late May)

Derby Hill Bird Observatory,
near Syracuse, New York
(March–May)

Ontario
*Niagara Peninsula, Beamer
Memorial Conservation
Area, Grimsby, Ontario
(March–mid-May)

Utah
*Jordanelle Reservoir,
near Heber City, Utah
(late February–early May)

Spring and Fall Sites
Minnesota
*Hawk Ridge Nature
Reserve, Duluth, Minnesota
(March-May; mid-August–November)

New Jersey
Raccoon Ridge, near
Blairstown, New Jersey
(second half of April;
mid-August–mid-November)

Places to Visit to See Live Raptors

CANADA
Alberta
Alberta Birds of Prey Centre
P.O. Box 1150
Coaldale, Alberta, T1M 1M9
Canada
413-345-4262
www.info@burringowl.com

Medicine River Wildlife
  Centre
P. O. Box 115
Spruce View, Alberta,
Canada T0M 1V0
403-728-3467
www:mrwrc@telusplanet.net

British Columbia
Kamloops Wildlife Park
P.O. Box 698
Kamloops, B. C., Canada
V2C 5L7
250-573-3242
www.info@kamloops
  wildlife.org

UNITED STATES
Alabama
Alabama Wildlife
  Rehabilitation Center
1926 Highway 31 S. #101,
Birmingham, AL 35244
205-320-6189
www.alawildliferehab.org

Treetop Nature Trail
Alabama Wildlife Center at
  Oak Mountain
100 Terrace Dr.
Pelham, AL 35124
205-663-7930
www.alawildliferehab.org

California
The Lindsay Wildlife
  Museum
1931 First Ave.
Walnut Creek, CA 95496
925-935-1978
www.wildlife-museum.org

The Wildlife Waystation
14831 Little Tunjunga
  Canyon Rd.
Angeles National Forest, CA
  91342-5999
818-899-5201
www.waystation.org

Colorado

Greenwood Wildlife
  Rehabilitation Sanctuary
P.O. Box 18987
Boulder, CO 80308
303-545-5849
www.greenwoodwildlife.org

Hawkquest
12238 N. 2nd St.,
Parker, CO 80134
303-690-6959
www.hawkquest.org

Florida

Wildlife Sanctuary of
  Northwest Florida
105 North "S" St.,
Pensacola, FL 32505
850-433-9453
wildlife105@juno.co
http://home.home.att.net/~
  ecase/wildlife

Georgia

Wildlife Rehabilitation
  Sanctuary
435 Cougar Lane
Eillijay, GA 30540
706-276-2980
www.wildliferehabsanctu
  ary.org

Idaho

World Center for
Birds of Prey
566 W Flying Hawk Lane
Boise, ID 83709
208-362-8687
medson@peregrinefund.org

Illinois

Henson Robinson Zoo
1100 East Lake Dr.
Springfield, IL 62707
217-753-6217
www.hensonrobinsonzoo.org

Maine

A. E. Howell Conference and
  Nature Center
Lycette Rd.
North Amity, ME 04471-9601

Minnesota

Audubon Center of the
  North Woods
P.O. Box 530
Sandstone, MN 55072
320-245-2648
Audubon1@ecenet.com

Quarry Hill Nature Center
  and Park
701 Silver Creek Rd., NE
Rochester, MN 55906
507-281-6114
www.rochester.k12.mn.us/
  quarryhill/home.htm

Wildlife Science Center
5463 W. Broadway Ave.
Forest Lake, MN 55025
651-464-3993
www.info@wildlifescience
  center.org

Minnesota Zoo
13000 Zoo Blvd.
Apple Valley, MN 55124
800-366-7811
www.mnzoo.com

Missouri

Clarksville Nature Awareness
  Center
Clarksville, MO 63336
573-242-3132
www.worldbirdsanctuary.
  org/clarks

Montana

Montana Raptor
  Conservation Center
P.O. Box 4061
Bozeman, MT 59772
406-585-1211
http://153.90.193.41/BigSky
Wildcare

New Jersey

The Raptor Trust, 1390
White Bridge Rd.,
Millington, NJ 07946
908-647-2353
www.theraptortrust.org

Woodford Cedar Run
  Wildlife Refuge, Inc.
4 Sawmill Rd.
Medford, NJ 08055
856-983-326
www.cedarrun.org

New York

Berkshire Bird Paradise
43 Red Pond Rd.
Petersburgh, NY 12138
(518) 279-3801
www.birdparadise.com

Hudson Valley Raptor
  Center,
South Road
Stanfordville, NY 12581
914-758-6957
www.net/~hvraptors/sched-
ule/html

Wild Spirit Rehab and
  Release Center
11511 Bixby Hill Rd.
Delevan, NY 14042-9642
716-492-3223
www.wildspirit.org

North Carolina

The Carolina Raptor Center
P.O. Box 16443 (Sample Rd.),
Charlotte, NC 28297
704-875-6521
http://birdsofprey.org/

Western North Carolina
  Nature Center
75 Gashes Rd.
Ashville, NC 28805
828-298-5600
  www.wildwnc.org/af/
  index.html

Oregon

Cascades Raptor Center,
32275 Fox Hollow Rd.
Eugene, OR 97405
541-485-1320
www.raptor-center.com

Oregon Zoo
4001 SW Canyon Rd.
Portland, OR 97221
503-226-1561
www.oregonzoo.org

Vermont

Vermont Raptor Center
27023 Church Hill Rd.
Woodstock, VT 05091
802-457-2779
www.vinsweb.org

Wisconsin

Wildlife Learning Center
N1750 State Rd. 22,
Wautoma, WI 54982
www.mecanriver.com

Selected Organizations

Hawk Migration Association
  of North America
c/o Mark Blauer
164½ Washington St.
Carbondale, PA 18407-2483

HawkWatch International
1800 S. West Temple,
  Suite 226
Salt Lake City, UT 84115

The International Osprey
  Foundation, Inc.
P. O. Box 250
Sanibel Island, FL 33957-0250

National Foundation to
  Protect America's Eagles
P.O. Box 333
Pigeon Forge, TN 37868

Northeast Hawkwatch
c/o Seth Kellogg
377 Loomis St.
Southwick, MA 01077

The Peregrine Fund, Inc.
World Center for Birds
  of Prey
566 West Flying Hawk Lane
Boise, ID 83709

Public Banding Demonstrations

Many sites across North
America do public banding
demonstrations. Here are
just a few:

Hawk Hill, Golden Gate
  Raptor Observatory
Bldg. 201, Fort Madison
San Francisco, CA 94123
415-331-0730
www.ggro.org

Holiday Beach
  Conservation Area
360 Fairview Ave.
West, Essex, ON N8M 1Y6
Canada
519-776-5209
callsop@erca.org

Effigy Mounds National
  Monument
151 Highway 76
Harpers Ferry, IA
319-873-3491
http://www.silosandsmoke
  stacks.org

Idaho Bird Observatory
Department of Biology
Boise State University
1910 University Dr.
Boise, ID 83725
208-426-3262
www.idbsu.edu/biology/ibo

Whitefish Point Bird
  Observatory
16914 N. Whitefish Point Rd.
Paradise, MI 49768
906-492-3596
www.wpbo.org

Hawk Ridge Nature Reserve
c/o Biology Department
University of Minnesota
Duluth, MN 55812
(218) 724-0261
www.hawkridge.org

Hawk Mountain Sanctuary
1700 Hawk Mountain Rd.
Kempton, PA 19529-9449
610-756-6000
www.hawkmountain.org

Braddock Bay Raptor
  Research
432 Manitou Beach Rd.
Hilton, NY 14468
716-392-5685
www.bbrr.com

Cape May Bird Observatory
Cape May Point, NJ 08212
609-861-0700
Birding hotline :
609-861-0466
www.njaudubon.org

A Sampling of Websites

http://birding.about.com/library/weekly/aa092499.htm
Hazel Bazemore Hawk Watch: Track hawks as they migrate down the Texas coastline to Central and South America, then click on the link to view the number of hawks that have been counted thus far this year. Results from previous hawk watches are also available.

http://birding.about.com/cs/camsnesting/index.htm or
http://birds.cornell.edu/birdhouse/camintro
Want to take a private peek into the nest of a raptor? This site will give you links to nesting raptors from eagles to owls. Keep a journal of what is happening every day and you'll soon become an "expert" on that particular nest.

http://birding.about.com/msub1-owls.htm
www.owlpages.com
These two sites will give all the information about owls that you could ever want plus photos, clip art, and puzzles of all sorts.

http://migratorybirds.fws.gov/pamphlet/house.html
Want to attract an owl to your backyard? This site will tell you all the stuff you need to know in order to be a good landlord, including designs and patterns for different nestboxes. It also discusses how you can protect habitat for birds.

www.ai-design.com/stargig/raptor/global/content/report/long-earedowl
Getting into raptors big time? This site provides you with instructional packets for hawks, owls, and falcons. Surprise your science teacher and share your interest: download a copy.

http://donb.photo.net/malheur/birds/seowl.html
Live in Oregon or taking a trip to that state, especially to the Mulheur National Wildlife Refuge? This site will provide you with specific directions on how and where to find an owl depending on the time of year.

www.peregrine-foundation.ca/programs.html
Track and observe nesting Peregrine Falcons. Watch them take their first flight and see where they go. These birds have transmitters to let you and scientists follow them.

www.mdbirds.org/mdbirding/finder/nosawwhet.html
Saw-whet Owls are fascinating little guys. If you live in Maryland or are passing through, check this site for directions to where Saw-whets can be found.

www.adoptabird.org
Want to do something good for raptors? Adopt-a-raptor is the perfect solution. Maybe your class in school would be interested in this project. Not only will you be helping very important members of our ecosystem but also you'll learn all about them.

http://birdsource.cornell.edu/bwha/
Follow Broad-winged Hawk migrations in fall and spring by clicking onto this site. It's almost as good as being there!

www.delta-education.com
Go to this site to order owl pellets, videos, field guides, and more.

Selected References and Reading

Bird Field Guides

Griggs, Jack L. *All the Birds of North America.* Harper Collins, 1997

Kaufman, Kenn. *Birds of North America.* Houghton Mifflin, 2000

National Geographic Society. *Field Guide to the Birds of North America,* 3rd Edition. National Geographic Society, 1999

Peterson, Roger T. *Eastern Birds.* Houghton Mifflin, 2002

Peterson, Roger T. *Western Birds.* Houghton Mifflin, 1990

Sibley, David A. *Sibley Guide to Birds.* Alfred A. Knopf, 2000

Stokes, Donald and Lillian Stokes. *Stokes Field Guide to Birds: Eastern Region.* Little, Brown & Co., 1996

Stokes, Donald and Lillian Stokes. *Stokes Field Guide to Birds: Western Region.* Little, Brown & Co., 1996

Raptor & Nest Identification

Dunne, Pete, David Sibley and Clay Sutton. *Hawks in Flight. The Flight Identification of North American Migrant Raptors.* Houghton Mifflin, 1988

Dunne, Pete, Debbie Keller, Rene Kochenberger. *Hawk Watch: A Guide for Beginners.* Cape May Bird Observatory, 1999

Harrison, Hal H. *A Field Guide to Birds' Nests in the United States East of the Mississippi River.* Houghton Mifflin, 1975

Harrison, Hal H. *A Field Guide to Western Birds' Nests in the United States West of the Mississippi River.* Houghton Mifflin, 1979

Sutton, Patricia and Clay Sutton. *How to Spot an Owl.* Chapters Publishing Ltd., 1994

Sutton, Clay and Patricia Taylor Sutton. *How to Spot Hawks & Eagles.* Chapters Publishing Ltd., 1996

Wheeler, Brian K. *A Photographic Guide to North American Raptors.* Academic Press, 1999

Wheeler, Brian K., and William S. Wheeler. *Peterson Field Guide: Hawks.* Houghton Mifflin, 1987

Natural History & Behavior

Bent, Arthur C. *Life Histories of North American Birds of Prey Part 1.* Dover, 1961

Bent, Arthur C. *Life Histories of North American Birds of Prey Part 2.* Dover, 1961

Brett, James J. *The Mountain and the Migration. A Guide to Hawk Mountain.* Cornell University Press, 1991

Breining, Grey. *Return of the Eagle: How America Saved its National Symbol.* Falcon Publishing, 1994

De la Torre, Julio. *Owls: Their Life and Behavior.* Crown, 1990

Erlich, Paul R., David S. Dobkin, and Darryl Wheye. *The Birder's Handbook: A Field Guide to the Natural History of North American Birds.* Simon & Schuster, 1988

Gessner, David. *Return of the Osprey.* Algonquin Books, 2001

Johnsgard, Paul A. *North American Owls: Biology and Natural History.* Smithsonian Institution Press, 1997

Poole, A. and F. Gill, Eds. *The Birds of North America.* The Academy of Natural Sciences and The American Ornithologists' Union

Sibley, David A. *Sibley's Guide to Bird Life and Behavior,* Alred A. Knopf, 2001

Stokes, Donald. *A Guide to the Behavior of Common Birds.* Little, Brown and Company, Stokes, Donald and Lillian. 1989. *A Guide to Bird Behavior, Vol. 3.* Little, Brown and Company, 1979

Weidensaul, Scott. *Living on the Wind. Across the Hemisphere with Migratory Birds.* Farrar, Straus and Giroux, 1999

Books for Young Birders

Jarvis, Kila and Denver W. Holt. *Owls: Who are They?* Mountain Press, 1996

Sattler, Helen Roney. *Book of North American Owls.* Clarion Books, 1995

Other

Broun, Maurice. *Hawks Aloft: The Story of Hawk Mountain.* Hawk Mountain Sanctuary Association, 1949

Connor, Jack. *Season at the Point: The Birds and Birders of Cape May.* Atlantic Monthly Press, 1991

Erickson, Laura. *Sharing the Wonder of Birds with Kids.* Pfeifer-Hamilton, 1997

Snyder, Noel and Helen. *The California Condor.* Academic Press, 2000

Weidensaul, Scott. *The Raptor Almanac: A Comprehensive Guide to Eagles, Hawks, Falcons, and Vultures.* The Lyons Press, 2000

Winn, Marie. *Red-Tails in Love: A Wildlife Drama in Central Park.* Vintage Books, 1998

Videos

Godfrey, Michael and Kenn Kaufman. *Owls Up Close,* 1991

Nature Science Network. *Hawks Up Close.* Nature Science Network, 1992

Walton, Richard K. and Greg Dodge. *Hawkwatch: A Video Guide to Eastern Raptors,* 1998

Wild Resource Conservation Fund, Harrisburg, PA. *American Kestrel: Finding a Home*

Wild Resource Conservation Fund, Harrisburg, PA. *Return From Forever* (Osprey Reintroduction Program)

Photo Credits

Index

Page numbers in **bold** indicate profiles of raptors.